core church communications
a series of basic publications and traini
Effective Church Communications
www.effectivechurchcom.com

Connection Cards

connect with visitors, grow your church, pastor your people—
little cards, big results

by

Yvon Prehn

published by

Effective Church Communications

Published by:
Effective Church Communications
www.effectivechurchcom.com
Ventura, California

Connection Cards, connect with visitors, grow your church, pastor your people—little cards, big results

For situations where you need formal permission, interviews with Yvon Prehn, or information about the ministry of Effective Church Communications, please go to www.effectivechurchcom.com or email: yvon@effectivechurchcom.com.

Cover art from stock.xchng, artist Billy Alexander, www.sxc.hu/profile/ba1969. This gentleman does incredible work. He is available for free-lance work and his contact email is: billyfalexander@bellsouth.net. Cover design by Yvon Prehn.

Previous versions of bits and pieces of this material have appeared in other books, articles, and on my website: www.effectivechurchcom.com.

Scripture versions and citations:
Unless otherwise noted, Bible verses are from the New International Version. Scripture taken from the HOLY BIBLE, NEW INTERNATIONAL VERSION®. Copyright © 1973, 1978, 1984 International Bible Society. Used by permission of Zondervan. All rights reserved.

Scripture quotations marked NLT are taken from the Holy Bible, New Living Translation, copyright 1996. Used by permission of Tyndale House Publishers, Inc., Wheaton, Illinois 60189. All rights reserved.

Passages marked (MSG) are taken from The Message translation.
Scripture taken from *The Message*. Copyright: 1993, 1994, 1995, 1996, 2000, 2001, 2002. Used by permission of NavPress Publishing Group.

Passages marked (KJV) are from the Kings James Version of the Bible. The King James Version is in the public domain in the United States.

He that is faithful in that which is least is faithful also in much: and he that is unjust in the least is unjust also in much.
(Luke 16:10, KJV)

It has long been an axiom of mine that the little things are infinitely the most important.
Sir Arthur Conan Doyle, aka Sherlock Holmes

"Not by might nor by power, but by my Spirit," says the LORD Almighty.
(Zac. 4.6)

Contents

author's note:

For many years I traveled all over North America giving seminars to literally thousands of church communicators to encourage and equip them to create effective church communications and to help their churches fully fulfill the Great Commission. Though I did some writing during that time, it was very difficult to travel and write.

Times have changed and so much can now be done online with live webinars, web-based training, teaching and resources. In addition to the great technology, not having to spend hours in boarding lines or recovering from Dramamine gives me many more hours in the day to write and create training materials.

And that's what I'm doing—creating training materials that are available to you 24/7—books, CDs, e-books, templates, all the training materials I've prayed for and dreamed about doing for years at my home in Ventura, California.

I'm sharing this because I wrote some of the materials while traveling and doing live seminars and I talk about them in the present tense in this book. I felt it would end up sounding somewhat stilted and awkward if I tried to change all of the references, so I left them in. I trust this brief explanation clarifies that I am no longer doing live seminars, though what I learned from them still applies.

ABOUT THIS UPDATE: I have corrected a number of typos and outdated references in this update, HOWEVER, correcting the quality of many of the scans in this book will have to wait until the next update. I wish they were better, but because of time and money limitations I'm not able to do them now. I trust the value of the written content will make up for that until they can be redone.

Connection Cards

Strategy

Connection cards might seem like a minor tool in your strategic plan to win your world to Jesus and to help your people grow in their Christian faith, but in reality they are one of the most powerful tools you have *if you take the time to learn to use them correctly.* That's what this book is all about.

Section 1: Strategy will set the strategic and biblical framework for an effective ministry with connection cards and will teach you:

- What connection cards can do for your church.

- What not to do for a successful connection card ministry, including some treasured "we've always done it this way" systems that may need to change.

- How to get the largest number of people to fill out and turn in connection cards.

- Suggestions on how to integrate paper-based connection cards with the new digital tools of connection: Twitter, Facebook, the web.

- How to respond to visitors in a structured and timely way, using the military and medical model of triage.

- How to use Church Management Software to help you do your job of recording connection cards and some cautions on its limitations.

- Fun and practical ideas for visitor follow-up using the connection cards as your starting point.

- How to use connection cards for prayer requests.

Section 2: Production will give you follow-up strategy suggestions with some nuts and bolts advice on how to implement a successful connection card ministry at your church with:

- Practical advice on how to create the cards along with mistakes to avoid.

• A gallery of examples of cards from real churches.

• Software recommendation for creating connection cards.

• Hardware suggestions for cost-effective print production.

• Finally, how to stay motivated in the ministry of connection cards by keeping your eyes on the eternal destiny of the people you can reach when you create, promote, record, and follow up on them effectively.

The importance of connection cards cannot be overstated, as the subtitle of the book says, connection cards will: *connect with visitors, grow your church, and pastor your people,* they truly are: *little cards with big results.*

Let's begin our journey to learn to use them effectively.

CHAPTER ONE

Introduction: though often overlooked, these little cards can accomplish great things

In church communications, we are often like Elijah when he waited on the mountain to meet with God. We expect him to act through the thunder and storm similar to the flashy multimedia popular today. Though God often uses the great, impressive tools of multimedia we have, he also uses tools that are similar to how he ultimately spoke to Elijah—through a still small voice.

Do the smallest things with the greatest love for God.

Mother Teresa

The place of connection cards in your church communication ministry is similar. They may appear tiny and unimportant in the great scheme of multimedia church communications available, but if you don't use them correctly, your church will probably not connect with visitors, grow, or meet the pastoral needs of your members as effectively as it will if you make the most of connection cards.

You can reach out, but if people don't reach back you haven't connected

We don't create these cards to wow people with great graphic design or to provide something for kids to scribble on during the church service. They are created to make a connection and connecting people to God and each other is what the church is all about.

For example, it is a few weeks from Easter as I write this and in my seminars, webinars, and on my website, I've suggested all sorts of communications in print and online that churches can create to connect with visitors to tell them about the church and to invite and encourage them to return. But helpful as they are, they fall short in one area. Their shortcoming is that all of them require the person *to come back to you.*

They can be created in a variety of styles, as the two cards on this page illustrate, but what is most important is not how they look, but what they do.

You can't reach back to visitors if you don't know they are there. You have no idea how they responded to the message or your church. You have no idea if they have a question you can answer or a hurt you can help to heal. Your congregation can be awed by your special music, but if they have no way to connect back to you, you might not know that a family lost their home last week, that a single parent needs prayer to keep looking for a job, or the joy of a father when a daughter or son is home safe from deployment overseas.

Connection cards are in many ways the foundation of all other communications in the church. They are often what starts the interaction between your church and a visitor; they are often what keeps the relationship going with members once they join your church.

The Bible reminds us that faithfulness in small things is very important to our Lord.

Though these communication pieces seem little, in many ways they are the foundation for everything else you do in your church.

This publication will give you:

· a vision for why you need to take the time to create these cards

· how to make sure you get a maximum response from them

· how to follow up in ways that will grow your church and minister to the needs of your people

This book will provide detailed instructions and practical advice from the many years I have worked with church communicators, evaluated and collected many cards, discussed their use with people who have attended my seminars, as well as personally using them extremely effectively in the various ministries my pastor husband and I have led.

If you carefully go over these materials and prayerfully apply them, I truly believe you will be astounded at how God take a seemingly little thing and use it greatly to grow your church and ministry to your people.

Though this book contains quite a bit of material on this topic, there is additional related material and more training on it on www.effectivechurchcom.com and on the training CD available at www.lulu.com/yvonprehn.

Before we begin, let's agree on a name

You are probably already using these communication pieces in some form. They are found in many places and go by a number of names and formats including:

· Friendship booklets or pads

· Connection cards

· Communication cards

· Visitor cards

· Prayer request forms

· Feedback cards

· A response form on your website

· Or they may not have a name of their own, but may be part of the Sunday church bulletin or worship folder and consist of a tear-off section.

No matter what their name, the purpose of this communication piece is the same: to get information from visitors and church members so the church staff can contact, pray for, or otherwise follow up with these folks.

No matter what their name, the purpose of this communication piece is the same: to get information from visitors and church members so the church staff can contact, pray for, or otherwise follow up with these folks.

Though the name of this communication piece can be whatever your church chooses to call it, we'll refer to it primary as a **connection card**. It is useful to have a consistent name for the purposes of this book, but the name itself is not really critical.

Another name that is often useful is **communication card**. Some churches like that because it has the idea of continuing communication between the church staff and the people in the pews. One more name that I have found very useful in the cards that I currently create is **feedback card**. Feedback is such a popular thing today with many business and media outlets constantly asking for your feedback. Particularly if you have a small church, house church or emergent church, referring to this process as feedback might work well.

The name itself is not critical, pick what works best for your people, your demographics, culture, and church setting. Again, in this book the majority of the time I will refer to the cards as connection cards, but sometimes as communication or feedback cards.

No matter what the name, keep the purpose foremost

We don't create these cards to wow people with great graphic design or to provide something for kids to scribble on during the church service. They are created to make a connection and connecting people to God and each other is what the church is all about.

Note to church planters or to pastors whose churches seem stalled in your growth:

TRY CONNECTION CARDS!

You will be amazed at how effective they can be to grow a church.

We must keep this important goal in mind of why we are having people fill out the connection cards, because having people fill them out is often viewed as an unnecessary interruption to the Sunday morning service. Recording, responding to, and dealing with them is often a bother on Monday.

In contrast to these attitudes, as briefly stated in the above introduction, it is important to emphasize that connection cards can:

· have a HUGE impact on growing your church

· connect people to the life of your church

· care for and address spiritual needs in practical ways

· and help your people grow to spiritual maturity

My purpose in creating this publication is to help you move past looking at these cards as merely ministry routine paperwork and to help you see them as essential tools to grow your church and change lives.

If you don't initially connect with visitors or with your people on an ongoing basis, nothing else your church does will have any impact on them. You can have the greatest follow-up program, a life-changing discipleship system, small groups that meet every need, but if a visitor quietly slips in and out and no connection is made, or if a frequent attendee attends Sunday only, no ministry you have will touch them.

People's needs remain the same no matter what media channel they use to communicate.

Your job is to use and respond to what is used most with your target audience.

If your people come to church week after week and don't know how to share their hurts, if they want to be part of a ministry but don't know how to connect, if your church needs volunteers and doesn't seem to be getting responses— your church can stall in its growth and your people won't mature in their faith. Connection cards, when used properly and effectively (and that is what this book will help you do) will solve these problems.

Before we begin practical advice, a few additional bits of introductory information might be useful.

Multimedia application

We are in the midst of a communication revolution. It wasn't many years ago that the ability to print inexpensively on cardstock at the church and in color would have been impossible. To record and respond to members with the power of database church management software was something only very large churches or corporations could afford. Now some versions are free on the web.

In addition to the advances in cheap printing and church database management, some churches today communicate to newcomers and members through their website, email, or cell phones. Some churches use Twitter and have Facebook groups; some churches have no idea what these tools are.

No matter where your church is on the scale of adapting new technologies, we know there will always be something new. We have no idea what communication tool will be the latest and greatest next. And no matter what is cutting edge at any moment, there will still be people in every church who we need to connect with in ways that seem outdated or old-fashioned. Though we don't know what the next tool will be, we both must stay open to new communication channels as well as maintain older ones for the sake of people who need them.

We live in the time of multi-channel communications, a time of both/and, not either/or in our communications in every area of the church. Though there is much else that can be said on this topic, our focus here is on connection cards. My church communicator's training site www.effectivechurchcom.com, has a lot of information and training on the various channels under the topic "multi-channel communication."

The bottom line is that people's needs don't change simply because they share a prayer request via an email connection or on a piece of paper and neither should our response to them. Though the exact mechanics vary, I've attempted in this book to provide advice that will apply whether your connection card is in print or in a digital format.

If there is an important distinction in how to respond using multimedia, or some multi-channel tip that I think might be useful I'll mention it, but mostly I'm trusting my readers to apply the communication principles I'm presenting to their churches in print and digital formats.

Most likely very few of you reading this book will have any formal training in communication creation, marketing, or many of the other skills helpful for successful church communications.

Be gentle on yourself and others as you read or see less than perfect work—we are all learning.

Note on examples, stories used throughout the book.

All of the stories and examples used in this book are true; they are not made up. However, because many of these illustrate what not to do, some details have been altered so as not to embarrass any specific member of the body of Christ. The details are altered, but the emotional pain and spiritual disappointment experienced by those who shared these stories with me is all too real.

One more thing about the stories: I have traveled all over the U.S. and Canada teaching and looking at church communications. I have visited many churches.

The mistakes and missteps, the shortcomings to effectiveness are the same everywhere. I'm saying this to those with a tender heart who may think I'm talking about your church in every example. Even if it seems like I'm talking about you, I'm probably not. Relax and realize we are all pilgrims, we are all learning how to communicate the words of eternal life in ways that are winning, winsome, and effective. Only our Leader is perfect.

We all make mistakes; we all fall short, but Lord willing, we can use these times as lessons and grow from them.

CHAPTER TWO

What connection cards can do for your church

People come to our churches every week—but tragically, depending upon which studies you look at, between 70-90% do not return.

Often we don't even know they were there. The pastor or membership committee can't respond to a visitor, tell them about the church, or invite them to an informational event or Bible Study unless *they give us* contact information. The connection card is the primary way to get this information during the church service.

Connection cards can stop people disappearing out the back door before we even know they came in the front door.

The connection card is also a vital link between the ministries the church has to offer and the people needing them. In addition to the connection with visitors, current church members may be involved in a difficult life situation, but they may not know who to call or how to share their burden. The pastoral staff may be unavailable or occupied with another personal crisis after the service. The member may not know who else to talk to and a critical personal need may remain unmet. The connection card can provide a way to communicate the need or a prayer request to the staff or prayer team outside of the Sunday morning service.

Why they work so well

No matter how secular, cynical, or postmodern our society is today, when a tragedy strikes, either community-wide or personal, people go to church.

Sometimes they don't even know why they picked a particular church. Often they don't know what to do when they get there—do they introduce themselves to someone? Who do they go to for questions? Who can provide help? They may have no idea what to do once there to get needs met or questions answered. But if they are intentionally given a card, asked to give feedback, to write down contact information, prayer requests or questions, they will.

A real-life example

For a number of years my husband and I led a Single Adult ministry at church in Southern California. We started with less than a handful of people, but in a couple of years had over 300 single adults involved. There were a number of reasons for this, but one of the main ways we grew as quickly as we did was because of the way this church used connection cards in the church service and how we used a version of them in our ministry itself. I'll explain briefly how this worked and the rest of this publication will fill out the process in more detail.

The church collected the cards on Sunday morning (again, how this was done will be explained in more detail later because the exact process is very important). Then my husband, Paul, who was the Single Adult Pastor, would get them on Monday morning and would follow up and make a connection with the Singles who visited. In the case of the singles, almost every week we would get at least one card that said something like this:

"I have been married for twenty years. My spouse just walked out on me and I don't know what to do."

My husband would call, make a connection, and invite the person to the Singles' Group. If possible, at least one other person from the group would also make a contact and invite them to come.

Each week in our Single Adult class itself, we would hand out a simplified version of the cards (there are examples of these in the Gallery section of this publication). This gave the person a continuing way to share needs, questions, and prayer requests. The cards were then copied and given out to the Singles' prayer team. In addition, my husband would literally carry the cards with him during the week to pray for his people.

It wasn't everything, but it was the start of a relationship

In addition to the opportunity to make that first, vital contact, on a continuing basis the cards enabled us to know week-by-week where our people were emotionally and spiritually.

We did many things to connect with Single Adults and grow them to Christian maturity, but the connection cards were a vital link to first link singles to the church and to us. Without them, many singles might have come to the church and not have known what to do with their pain. It's unlikely a newly separated single person would go up to and usher and say, "I haven't been alone since high school and I'm terrified." That person would also probably not write down on a friendship pad for all to see, "My husband just walked out on me." But the connection cards, if done properly, give an opportunity for someone to share their pain and then for the church to make a connection and help heal a life.

In addition to the opportunity to make that first, vital contact, on a continuing basis the cards enabled us to know week-by-week where our people were emotionally and spiritually. We did not have time to meet, touch base with, and chat with each person every week, but we did have time to read their prayer cards. Sometimes people don't even want to talk about on-going problems, but need on-going prayer. When necessary, we were also able to follow up with a phone call or email after reading the cards.

Briefly, that is how we have used the connection cards in a specific ministry. More will be said in a later section on how to follow up after collecting the cards on a church-wide basis.

Before reading any further, a commitment must be made

This important commitment, which I'll detail shortly, moves beyond the obligatory paperwork and record-keeping most churches do with their connection cards. All churches capture, or attempt to capture the following information with their connection cards:

· name and contact information from visitors

· information about regular attendees and members

· response to the message, including calls to trust Jesus as Savior or to commit to a life change or new spiritual direction

· responses to requests for volunteer positions

· sign-up information for church events

· prayer requests

These are wonderful, valid reasons to use connection cards, but it's what is done with them after the information above is collected that makes them an important tool in your church or ministry and life-changing to the people who give you the information. As the example of the Single Adult Ministry illustrated, connection cards served as a vital tool to connect with hurting people and enfold them into the church community.

To make their use successful, the church staff must commit to a vision that sees how these humble pieces of paper or cardstock can literally change the life or the eternal destiny of a person.

A process similar to what we did with singles can be replicated through every area of the church and most importantly in the church itself overall. But to make their use successful, the church staff must commit to a vision that sees how these humble pieces of paper or cardstock can literally change the life or the eternal destiny of a person. It is a vision that sees connection cards, not as simply an administrative bother to be quickly dispensed with during the service and entered into church databases whenever there is down time during the week, but to see them as a vital link between your church and:

· a visitor who may be in incredible emotional pain from a loss

· an honest seeker who wants to know more about God

· a church member who has questions or is hurting

· anyone who has a prayer request that is easier to confidentially share in writing than to verbalize

The connection card is the vital, practical link to make the connections possible. This vision to see what this humble communication can do and a conviction of its importance in the spiritual life of your church and your people is essential to give you the energy and persistence to do all the things you need to do to make your ministry with communication cards as successful as it can be.

Please pray for the Lord to give you and your church staff and communication team this vision because. . .

In addition to commitment to a vision, there is a big cost to effectively use connection cards

Digital duplicators can produce connection cards for fractions of a penny, so production cost is not an issue.

The cost isn't in money. There is very little tangible monetary cost to effectively print or use connection cards. Though these cards can work well with some of the excellent church management software programs available today (more on this later in the book) you don't need expensive software to make a huge change in the way your church uses these cards or in the effectiveness of the cards. Any church, any size, on a small budget or almost no budget, can use them to effectively grow and deepen their ministry.

The true cost of effectively using connection cards is in time commitment.

Any size church, on any budget can afford monetarily to have an effective connection card ministry.

The true cost in using communication cards effectively is in the time commitment you must make to them.

It takes time (and usually more than we planned) to:

· Create the cards

· Explain and announce them properly

· Give people time to fill them out

· Go over them and carefully enter the information into the church database

· Biggest cost of all—to respond to needs, questions, and volunteer sign-ups on the cards

All of this time is not easy to find. Your timely response to heartfelt needs expressed at crisis times is vitally important in the spiritual warfare for souls. You can be quite certain there will never seem to be time to do all the things need to be done. The enemy of our souls will whisper in your ear many reasons why you should be doing something else other than attending to connection cards. Knowing these challenges will come, count the cost up-front, because few things hurt people more or are more damaging to your church or leadership credibility than if you ask people to share their prayer requests and needs, but when they do, you don't make time to follow through on responding to them. The damage may be irreparable.

What a church commitment in vision and time to connection card ministry looks like:

It is essential the entire church staff has the same commitment to this ministry. If the pastor passionately presents connection cards and they are not followed up on or if there is committed follow up in place, but the cards are not presented clearly and so few are collected—if either link in the process fails, the connection card ministry will not have the impact it should.

· The staff, pastors, administrators, anyone involved with the cards has the same vision and commitment to them.

Achieving this common commitment is very important, because an effective ministry of connection cards must involve the entire staff if it is to be effective. If every staff member reads this book or even skims it, that can be helpful. Money for copies of the book is not an object because if you purchased this book as a download you have my permission to make copies of it (as many as you want) to pass along to staff or volunteers.

For those who are not readers, on my website: www.effectivechurchcom.com is a video that can be watched or listened to that goes over the basic concepts in this book. After everyone on staff has the opportunity to take in the basic information, then the following steps can be taken:

· Initially commit to considering all the suggestions in this book, pray about them, and discuss the strategy at staff meetings.

· Commit to having the resources on hand in the church, suggested in this book, for effective follow up.

· Commit the time and people (staff and volunteers) needed to respond so no expressed need is ignored, so all are dealt with in timely and appropriate ways.

· Commit to accountability in follow-up and follow-up schedules.

· Make the importance of connection cards part of your church membership classes so that new members understand that in filling them out each week they demonstrate to visitors how important they are. This will also help visitors want to fit in because they will be doing what everyone else does.

· Commit to pray for the connection card ministry regularly, that your church be clear and consistent in your use of them, that your follow up be faithful, and that the Lord honor that ministry by connecting people with your church and changing lives for eternity.

With proper commitments in place, let's get practical

Before I discuss the process that works best to create connection cards and to get people to fill them out and turn them in, it might be helpful to note some church practices I have observed that don't work particularly well.

What not to do in connection card ministry

"Because we've always done it that way."

Though that might be why you are using the particular method of collecting information from visitors and your people, consider, please consider doing things a new way if you find your current church practices described here.

I've been teaching church communications for over twenty years (more info on my background in the back of this book) and have looked at many connection cards and discussed their use with many church communicators during that time. From my experience, and many years of personally using them in a variety of church settings, I've found the following activities and tools don't contribute to maximum communication success in getting either initial contact or continuing ministry information from people.

I also realize that, though not the most successful, many of the following practices have been done by many churches for a long time and it is difficult to imagine doing things a different way. If that is your situation, please suspend defensiveness or judgment until you've finished this entire publication to see the recommendations that might replace these actions.

Change is always challenging and difficult and if your church does some of the things that follow, I appreciate your willingness to consider alternative ideas. After each suggestion of what not to do, I'll briefly list the alternative action as "a better idea," and after this section, the alternative actions will be discussed in more detail.

#1 Don't use "Friendship Pads/Booklets"

The privacy concerns of people today requires we modify how we collect information.

In some churches, much more so in the past than today, the procedure for capturing contact information from visitors and members involves a booklet with lined pages inside that is passed down the pew for people to fill in and then passed back down the pew to be collected by ushers. As it is passed back, the leader often recommends that people "Notice who is a visitor."

This tends not to work very well for visitors today. There are a number of reasons why, one of the main ones being the current privacy concerns of people. To many, this is simply too public a way to give out personal information.

Perhaps I am more sensitive to this because I work with single adults, but to a ask a single woman who visits your church to write down her name, address, phone number, email, and then pass it down a row of strangers, while adding that people make note of new people in the pew beside them—she probably won't do it. Most likely you don't have people in your church who will stalk or take advantage of a single woman alone, but the trust level towards the church or strangers, for many people today, men and women, is quite low.

These "Friendship Pads" may have worked well years ago when the world at least seemed to be a safer and more friendly place, but our world has changed. In additional to personal safety issues, privacy concerns and concerns about identity theft cause many visitors to pass them on without filling them out.

A better idea: a card that can be filled out, folded over, and personal information handed in without being made visible to others.

#2 Don't use a tear-off piece

There are several reasons for this—consider them carefully before discounting my comments, because this method is used in lots of churches and it seems like such a simple and easy way to collect information from visitors and regular church attendees. Unfortunately, it's not as simple as it seems.

First of all, if you primarily use connection cards to find out about visitors, keep in mind that study after study shows that visitors do not like to stand out. Being the one person in your row tearing out a piece of paper in an otherwise quiet church service is a rather loud operation and one guaranteed to turn heads in the visitor's direction. Few people want that to happen.

Minimize situations that make seekers stand out from the group and make them feel odd or unusual. Help them blend in to the group, to feel welcome and not different.

John Kamp

To avoid that situation, some churches have everyone "tear it off all together." That seemed like a good solution to me (it's what is done at the church we currently attend) until we brought to church a dear woman who had recently become a believer in her late 60s. As everyone was tearing off their form in church, I was watching her out of the corner of my eye and noticed she was having a rather difficult time grasping the flimsy paper. The arthritis in her hands made it difficult and after several tries, obviously embarrassed, she glanced around and tried to unobtrusively put the bulletin down beside her. Her connection card did not get turned in; no follow-up came from the church, and though she wouldn't really tell me why, she didn't want to come to our church again.

My heart hurt watching her and I thought if it makes one little lady embarrassed, if she can't communicate she was there and perhaps share a prayer request, maybe there are better ways to use a connections piece.

There are lots of little ladies in our world. People come to know Jesus and visit at church for the first time at many ages and with disabilities of varies types and we don't want our method of paper handling to get in the way of connecting with them.

A better idea: a separate connection card made of card stock that does not need to be torn out and that is easy to write on solves all of these problems. Specifics on how to create the card are discussed later.

#3 Don't tell people about connection cards without giving them time to fill them out.

This is probably the single biggest reason churches do not get connection cards turned in. In most churches, either the pastor or another church leader will mention the connection card very quickly in passing, often when people are still standing up after singing a song. Sometimes it will be mentioned when people are sitting down, but often then it is part of a long series of announcements and no time is given so people can actually fill it out.

The problem with this approach is that a visitor or church member, if they want to respond or turn in a prayer request, has to then decide when to quit paying attention to what is going on up front so they can fill out the card, for example:

· Do you want them to ignore part of the sermon?

· Write during the prayer time?

· Stay seated and scribble while an upbeat praise song is being sung?

· Juggle the elements while trying to write during communion?

Something has to be ignored while they read a card with which they are unfamiliar and fill it out.

A better idea: after telling people about the card; pause, play a few bars of music and give them time to actually fill it out. More detail on this process later.

#4 Don't tell people to take the connection cards to the visitor center to get a gift from the church

You might have a wonderful gift and fantastic people at your visitor center, but your response rate will be much less if people have to take extra steps or actions to get to where you want them to take a card, simply because a large number of people may forget or not be able to go there.

For most church visitors and members after the church service, the thought of a good meal or kids that need to be picked up is often much more appealing than a trip to the visitor center to drop off a connection card.

For example, if you are a visitor who has children to pick up from their first time in the nursery; if you are depressed and don't want to talk to anyone; if the idea of a CD of a message by the pastor isn't your idea of a gift you are interested in, or even if you or your spouse is simply really hungry and can't wait to get to brunch, there are all sorts of reasons why taking a connection card to a visitor center might not happen.

A better idea: pic the connection cards up as part of the offering. An extra benefit of this process is that visitors have something to put into the offering plate other than money, which is an added incentive to turn in their information.

#5 Don't take them up prior to hearing the message

One of the purposes of connection cards is for the church to find out how people respond to the sermon. If the sermon contains a challenge to serious life changes, an invitation to respond to personal salvation, a challenge to holy living or repentance, a call to sign up for small groups, or some spiritual growth program, the pastor needs to know if there is a response and the church staff needs to respond to the decision made for it to be more than a momentary emotional response.

The connection card is one of the best ways to make this connection, particularly in many churches where a call to "come forward" may make some people so uncomfortable it obscures the spiritual decision that needs to be made.

In the cards that I have looked at, I know many churches recognize this and have places where people can check statements such as:

___I trusted Jesus for my personal salvation today.

___I rededicated my life to Christ today.

___I commit to begin the Bible reading program with the church.

___I want to be part of a small group.

These are important responses for the church to know about, so an appropriate response back to them, confirming their commitments and telling the person what to do next can be made. Sadly, in looking at the order of service listed in many bulletins, I have found some churches take up the cards during the offering BEFORE the sermon has been preached. I know the stress of working in a church office can be overwhelming and that we sometimes don't take time to read through and think about what we print, but to ask people to respond to challenges, record a significant spiritual decision, and turn in the information BEFORE they hear the sermon, doesn't make any sense at all.

Better idea: move the taking up of the offering until after the sermon, so people have time to hear the message and challenge, to think about it, and let the church know of a well-thought out decision.

#6 Don't even think about looking at ways to make collecting your connection cards more effective if you are not committed to timely and appropriate follow up.

Though specifics on how to follow up will be discussed in detail later in this book, one of the most destructive things in a connection card ministry is lack of follow up.

Make a commitment to timely follow up from the start or nothing else you do with connection cards will be of value.

If you follow every procedure I recommend, you will get lots of cards turned in—for a few weeks. But if you do not follow up, it can poison the attitude of your congregation and of returning visitors.

If you passionately proclaim the need to fill out the cards because the church really wants to connect with "guests" and that volunteers for the upcoming event are vital to its success, *if you do not respond to the cards within a week, don't bother use them until you are able to follow up.*

The second time people hear your words and no response follows, they will be less likely to respond. If a number of weeks go by and people have turned in connection cards with visitor addresses and questions, prayer requests, or offers to volunteer, and they never receive a response from the church, a justifiable disappointment and perhaps a sad cynicism will silently filter through the congregation if pleas to fill out cards continue. Visitors will notice.

On the other hand, if your congregation fills out the cards with expectation and the joy of interacting with the staff and church family, visitors will catch those emotions also. They will want to be part of the interaction.

What not to worry about

In the previous listing of what not to do, you probably noticed that none of the things not to do had anything to do with how the card looked, the layout, the typeface, or graphics. Though these are important issues (we don't want something ugly, unreadable, or hard to fill out) how a card looks is more about the style and look of your church than it is a factor it the effectiveness of its use. In addition, many ideas and tips for the layout and production of connection cards will be given in the Production: Gallery section of this book.

What is more important, no matter the specific look of the card, is how you present it to get the largest number of people to fill it out, which the next section will discuss in detail.

CHAPTER FOUR

How to get the maximum number of connection cards turned in

How your card looks depends on the style, denomination, and location of your church. For example, the connection card from a Community Church in Southern California will most likely look very different than a connection card from a Lutheran church in Michigan. Any design can work, it's how you present it that is most important to assure a good response.

There are, no doubt, many ways to effectively use connection cards. The one following has been what I have personally experienced to be an extremely successful method in a variety of churches and ministry settings.

There are a number of seemingly little, picky steps in this procedure, but please do not discount them. What may seem like a tiny, unimportant procedure could actually be a turning point in the journey of a soul either to or away from connecting with your church and Jesus.

I apologize in advance for the churches that have a liturgy that would make this method unrealistic. My recent personal experiences in using this type of connection card and this procedure has come from non-liturgical churches. But I do know from the wonderful folks I interact with in my seminars, that no matter what your church worship format, if you truly want to connect with visitors and members, and if you are gripped by a vision of what connection cards can do, you will come up with creative ways to make it work, no matter what your liturgical format.

The following chapters on how to respond and use the cards after you collect them are the same for any church.

Whatever your church worship format, with what follows, feel free to use what is useful, and modify or improvise in any way to make it workable and appropriate for your church. Vary one or two things to see if the changes make a difference. Record what you try and record the response before the change and the results after the change.

Remember, the only measure of success in a church communication project, is how do people respond? The response that you are looking for is **how many fill out the cards and turn them in.** This connection with people is what matters.

No matter what procedure you use, especially if it is a new one, there will be people who won't like it. Young or old; some people will think they are unnecessary; some people won't want to change the way "things have always been done."

In advance prepare to gently explain that we are doing this to connect with people; that we are testing a new way and we will measure if this procedure will encourage more visitors to let us know they are there and if it helps our members response to us. People connecting with the church, not pleasing personal preferences is your North Star. Keep focused on it.

Before the announcement about the connection cards

Pew racks for connection cards are your distribution method of last resort. Requiring people to reach over someone, take them out of the rack, and then fill them out will greatly cut down on your response.

A few things need to be in place before an announcement can be made about the cards including:

· The cards have to be made up. For the form of the cards themselves, a separate card, printed on uncoated card stock works best. (See Gallery section for examples). A digital duplicator can print them very inexpensively.

· The cards themselves should be inserted into the weekly church bulletin or worship folder.

· If the church does not use or give out a church bulletin or worship folder at the start of the service, cards can be handed out or put in pew racks. Placement in pew racks however, often greatly cuts down on response.

Brief, true story here: after one of my seminars where we talked about the value of connection cards, a gentleman came up to me and asked, "How do you think the response rate would change if you put the cards into pew racks instead of having them in the bulletin?"

"You've already done that, haven't you?" I smiled and asked.

"Yes," he said sheepishly, "but tell me what do you think would happen?"
"I think the response would drop significantly," I answered.

"It went from good to zero," he said, "why do you think that happened?"

I honestly didn't know.

Even if your bulletin is printed on glossy paper stock, be sure to print your connection cards on uncoated paper using an ink, not toner-based printer.

You cannot write on glossy paper or toner-based images. More information on connection card production is in the back of the book.

I suggested, in a rather lame attempt at humor, that maybe people were so tired on Sunday that to have to lift a card out of the pew rack was more than they could handle. There could be many reasons, including the discomfort of perhaps having to reach over people to get to them. But reasons aside, I've seen his experience repeated many times in other churches.

Bottom line: if you have the cards in pew racks, and people have to reach over and get one to fill it out, response will be significantly decreased.

This is not to say that you cannot make this method work, but you have to take additional time to focus on the cards and train your people to perhaps take one out and hand it to a visitor or the person beside them.

· No matter where or how people get the cards, be sure the pew racks have pencils or pens with which to fill out the cards. Be sure the pencils or pens will actually write on the cards. Remember nothing writes very well on slick, glossy paper. If you have a slick, glossy printed bulletin you should have a separate card printed on uncoated stock for your connection card. Be sure to actually test writing on whatever you have printed.

Connection card announcement procedure

What the pastor or worship leader says will be printed in **Bold Italics** in the section that follows with explanatory notes interspersed.

Early in the service, when people are sitting down, the pastor or worship leader stands up and says:

"Would everyone please take out your connection card."

Everyone is asked to do this for several reasons.

· Cards can be used for taking church attendance, for use in filling in database church membership/management programs.

· Cards can be used for current member communication, for prayer requests, response to volunteer requests, attendance numbers at church events, etc.

· If everyone is filling out a card, the visitor will be motivated to do what everyone else is doing and will not feel uncomfortably singled out as they might if they were the only one in the row filling out the card.

· During membership classes, encourage your members to do this on a weekly basis and to encourage those around them to do it also.

Pastor or leader continues:
"If you are a visitor, please fill out your contact information. We would love to be in touch with you to tell you more about our church. If you are a regular attendee, just give us your name."

"Whoever you are, think of this as your feedback card or connection card to the church."

· It's up to you what you want to call it—whatever you are most comfortable with is what is important.

· One positive aspect of calling it a feedback card, or mentioning feedback as a use of the card, is that feedback in any form or situation is a very popular thing today. Television programs, websites, blogs, many forms of communication today all give us an opportunity for feedback.

· Depending upon your audience and the situation, you may want to add a disclaimer similar to what people see on websites and any area asking for information today, by saying something like:

"Any information shared is confidential and for the church staff only." (a longer disclaimer is in the Gallery Section)

· Continue an encouragement to get the card filled out by saying something like:

"We really want to hear from you. If you have a prayer request, if you have a question, if there is any way we can help or be of service to you on your spiritual journey, we want to know about it."

This procedure has been used extensively in a number of settings and is extremely successful in getting people to fill out and turn in connection cards.

ALL the steps are very important for maximum response.

· What happens next is the hardest thing of all and the most important.

· The pastor or the person who has introduced the cards needs to:

Pause, allow a few bars of music to be played and give people time to fill out the cards.

· If desired, the pastor or leader can say:

"I'm going to take time to fill out my card while all of you fill out your cards."

· The reason why this is so important is because it gives people time to actually fill out the card. They will not miss out on any part of the service by taking time to fill it out; they will not be distracted if they have a prayer request wondering when they are going to take time to fill out the card.

· I warn you—it will seem absolutely impossible to take time to do this. Test the number of seconds this takes, it will surprise you how few they are. Please remember, those few seconds can be life and eternity-altering.

· After giving people time to fill out the connection card, the pastor or leader can then say:

"Hold on to the cards during the rest of the service. We will collect them near the end with the offering. Again, let me encourage you, if at any time during the message if you have a question, or feedback—if there is something that I do that you don't like, we want to know."

· The service continues and after the sermon, near the end of the service, the pastor or church leader again stands up and says:

"Would you please take out your connection card. You've heard the sermon and now we want to hear from you. Again, if you have a prayer request, if you made a decision today, if you have a question about the teaching you heard or are confused about any part of our church service, if there is any way we can help you on your spiritual journey, we want to know.

"We'll be collecting the offering in a few minutes. If you are not a member of our church, please don't feel you have to contribute financially. The only contribution we want from you is the connection card."

The offering is now collected along with many connection cards.

What to do after you collect the connection cards

Getting the largest number of people to fill out connection cards is only the first step in using them for effective ministry. If you have followed the procedure above—**be prepared.**

You will be astounded at the number and variety of responses you receive.

To actually pause and give people time to fill out the connection card is one of the hardest things you will ever do but it is absolutely ESSENTIAL if you want the maximum number of people to fill out the cards and turn them in.

It only takes a few seconds—don't let the screaming voices in your head tell you you don't have time to do it.

You need to be prepared for this because nothing is worse than asking people to share personal information with the church, pour out their hearts, respond to a message offering salvation or life change, or volunteer for a challenging job around the church and then for your church to not respond.

When people fill out a connection form, it is like one person putting out their hand for someone to shake. If the person to whom the hand is offered doesn't reach out and take the offered hand, no connection takes place. People have put out their hand to the church in filling out the card; you must reach back with either a phone call, email, letter or personal contact, (more and detailed ideas on how to do later) because until you respond, the person who metaphorically put out their hand by filling out the card is left hanging, waiting.

It cannot be emphasized strongly enough that to not respond to connection cards in a timely and appropriate manner can be more damaging than not creating and passing them out in the first place.

When an offered handshake is refused or ignored, hurt feelings, rejection and misunderstanding take place. You may never know the courage it took for someone to take a first step towards Jesus or for them to ask for help. You won't feel the hope expressed in turning in the connection card that the church might really care, or the pain desperately shared in a simple prayer request. It cannot be emphasized strongly enough that to not respond to connection cards in a timely and appropriate manner can be more damaging than not creating and passing them out in the first place.

The next chapter contains important suggestions for your follow up. You might sigh a big sigh of relief when you get a great response when many visitors and members turn in the cards—but don't relax too soon—the real work has just started.

An optional way to get input in addition to your physical connection cards

Don't feel you have to do this, but for some churches, in some settings, consider:

Encourage visitors to send you text messages, Twitter responses, connect with your Facebook page, or whatever new technology is operational when you read this.

Use many of the same steps mentioned previously in that you take a time to focus on and encourage response and interaction.

For a very interesting example of how this kind of interaction can work, check out how many of the current television commentators respond to social media messages. Even while doing a newscast, some commentators have several computer monitors in front of them and are continuously asking questions and interacting with the messages that are sent to them via the web, Twitter, and Facebook in real time.

In many ways this is perhaps the opposite side of a continuum starting on one side with a highly structured liturgical church where every action is anticipated and predictable to a fluid, interactive, emergent or nontraditional church. There is no perfect system for every church or every outreach program. First and foremost always ask the Lord to help you see the needs and best ways to connect with the people you are called to reach.

Precedents in missions for cultural accommodation

In the early days of mission outreach to China, Hudson Taylor and Lottie Moon experienced great breakthroughs in response to the Christian message when they adopted Chinese dress. Learning the language was also vitally important, but so was dressing like the people dressed who they wanted to reach.

Chinese language and dress would not have been appropriate for outreach in America during that time, but for the people God called them to reach it was necessary and important.

Today, to be culturally relevant you may want to explore the most recent social media used by members of your congregation.

It may take a team

In some churches, a significant part of your congregation is already involved in texting while you are speaking—why not have someone, or a tech team who can engage them in spiritual conversations?

That previous suggestion may have struck fear into your heart if you are not active on social media. Don't worry, not every up-front communicator is multi-channel, multi-tasking skilled; nor does he or she need to be.

For years, churches have often had multiple people involved in conducting the church service, for example, someone is playing music while the preacher is giving an altar call or asking for a response. Altar boys and girls assist the pastor or priest in mass and liturgy.

Something to think about: Consider a tech minister, who responds to text messages, tweets, and other forms of digital communication while the preacher is preaching. That person could sit in the back, balcony, or in a place where their texting will not be a distraction to others. The text minister could answer questions, refer questions to websites for additional information, get names to follow up on later. The ministry possibilities are as wide as the web.

Please, if this totally scares you or seems wildly inappropriate, don't worry about it; this is not something for everyone. However, for some churches, who are reaching a younger or highly technical audience, you can rest assured that what you want to do is not heretical. There are many precedents in missionary history.

Other uses for social media

Using social media, especially Twitter during church services, is not necessary for most churches. But it is a useful tool for interactions outside of the church service.

On my website www.effectivechurchcom.com I am going to be doing additional articles and training on this. As I write, we are setting up some new things in our church I'll be reporting on as soon as I see how it goes.

PLEASE, if you are using any of the social media effectively in your church—and I don't mean simply have a Twitter and Facebook logo on your bulletin cover so you look cool—but if you are really using them in ministry, please email me at: yvon@effectivechurchcom.com, tell me your story and give me permission to share it. I'd love to put together a collection of ideas on how we can be effective cybermissionaries.

CHAPTER FIVE

How to respond effectively to connection cards, an overview

A lack of follow-up on collected connection cards will not only waste your efforts but have negative consequences.

At this point, the hard work of the connection card ministry is just starting. Before we get specific about how to respond, let's take a minute to review what we've learned so far.

Following the advice given in the previous chapter is important because I've found that people assume the look of their connection card is the primary determinate as to whether people fill them out or not. Though we want the design to be clear, the paper or card stock easy to write on, and enough space between lines to write easily, nothing matters in the design if the church procedures do not include intentional ways to be sure the maximum number of people fill out the cards.

As previously discussed these intentional actions include having the pastor or worship leader focus on the cards, explain them clearly, and giving people time to fill them out are extremely important. Finally, again encouraging people to fill them out and collecting them at the end of the service with the offering is a way to assure that a maximum number of cards will be collected.

All of the work described above is essential, but if you aren't ready and committed to follow up immediately with the requests and responses you receive on the cards, all of your efforts will not only be wasted, but will have negative consequences.

In the following sections are suggestions on what to have in place and what to do to make the whole process a positive, church-growing one.

Plan ahead on how to handle the requests and responses you will receive

When people are physically wounded they need immediate care. When people are spiritually wounded, a lack of response to a need or question expressed on a connection card may irreparably damage their hearts and openness to Jesus.

You shouldn't wait to figure out your response to people after you collect the cards any more than a battlefield medical team would have a staff meeting to figure out how to deal with the wounded as they are coming in. When people are bleeding, medical teams don't sit around and ask:

· "Do you think we need an operating room?"

· "Where are the bandages? I know we have some somewhere."

· "Who will administer, the IV? I think this person will die if they don't get one."

· "Do you think in the next couple of weeks you can set that broken leg?"

If a battlefield medical team was asking these questions, when they should be responding with action, we'd accuse them of incredible incompetence in dealing with the lives of the wounded.

Fortunately, that is not how battlefield wounded are treated. During the recent war, television news has shown numerous specials on the speed of treatment on the battlefields and the cutting-edge surgery and treatment teams available to help our troops.

For the emotionally and spiritually wounded who come to our churches each week and who fill out connection cards listing their needs, is your church able to respond immediately with concrete, useful answers?

Or are these questions sometimes asked in the church office:

"Did the prayer requests get typed up this week yet?"

· "We've got a food bank referral, don't we?"

"Who is doing hospital visitation this week?"

"What did we do with that pregnancy hot line number?"

"Who is answering the requests for information about the single's ministry?"

"Where is our list of small groups?"
· "Another death for a family member in our church family....oh, dear....where and when is that grief workshop being held?"

· "Did the connection cards get entered into the data base? It's Friday already and we don't want next week's piling up."

You need people and procedures in place before beginning a connection card ministry

None of the issues or needs expressed above should come as a surprise to any church staff. Though each situation is unique to some extent, overall people experience similar needs and the resources to meet them can be prepared ahead of time.

With that in mind, before you can begin to respond to your connection cards, PLEASE be sure you have all the needed people and procedures in place. Again, I cannot emphasize strongly enough that it is better to not even create the cards, than to have them, ask people to fill them out, and then ignore them. It is often said that you never get a second chance to make a good first impression. With connection cards, it may not be too strong to say that you will not get a second chance to connect or gain trust with a visitor or church member if you ignore their connection card or unreasonably delay your response to them.

Specific resources needed

You need the following three areas of response in place before you institute a connection card ministry:

· People Resources

· Spiritual Resources

· Social Service Resources

Let's now look at each of these resource areas in more detail:

People Resources: who will respond to the connection cards?

The answer is not automatic and will involve more than one person for the variety of responses needed. The answer does not stop with the administrative assistant whose job it is to sort and enter information on a database and/or prayer list.

The data entry is a clerical and administrative action done by an often already overworked person. In addition to the careful work required in recording, this person should not be responsible for the pastoral responses then needed.

One of the best resources for training a pastoral care team to respond to connection cards is the Stephen Ministries:
www.stephenministries.org

The person doing the data entry is involved in a ministry of recording and this is an honored and important ministry. As the books of Numbers and Chronicles in our Bibles remind us, the careful recording of God's people is of extreme importance. It is the basis for all other actions.

After the ministry of recording, other people, in addition to the pastors, who respond to specific pastoral requests, are needed for the ministry of connection. To assign these responsibilities, you need to decide such things as:

· Who will contact visitors and how?

· Who will contact people in crisis?

· Who will let people know we are praying for them?

· Who will follow up on volunteer requests?

In even a very small or starting church or ministry, it is best to have some sort of Pastoral Care team in place to respond to connection cards.

The pastor of the church will most likely be part of that team and there are some folks he or she may want to handle personally, but the majority of the responses to connection cards should be handled by a Pastoral Care Team.

I cannot recommend strongly enough that your church consider Stephen Ministries as a resource in setting up a Pastoral Care team to deal with the needs that will come to you through the connection cards. Stephen Ministries is a group that works with all denominations and all sizes of churches to train people in pastoral care. Please go to their website: www.stephenministries.org for more information about the organization, for training and useful resources.

At the very least, even without formal training, the church should have caring volunteers who can help to make follow up phone calls and emails for clarification, to answer questions, and to make referrals. This group might also be part of a visitation or visitor response team. More later how to use this team, but for right now, be sure there are people in place.

Spiritual Resources

The responses you have in place in this area may vary in some ways depending upon your church, its size, its location and the particular target groups you are trying to reach. For example, a large inner-city church may need different resources than a small rural church.

But regardless of your location, all churches need to be able to respond to the following spiritual issues (expressed in all sorts of ways) when people ask on their connection card:

· How do I become a Christian?

· How do I come back to God if I wandered away?

· How do I deal with an addiction or habit I can't control?

· Can God forgive my sins?

· Why does your church believe.......(many questions here)

· How do I become a member of this church?

· Can the church help me with my struggles with....(many issues here: addictions, loneliness, loss)?

You need to have responses in place that can be given to people in a variety of ways including:

· Some people will want a phone call. A caring, trained volunteer, pastor, or Stephen's minister would be the appropriate responder here.

· Some people may prefer to receive a letter. Be sure you have tracts, denominational literature, and church brochures that answer spiritual questions. The American Tract Society has an excellent collection of tracts that answer many spiritual questions. They are available at *www.atstracts.org*

· Others may indicate they prefer to be contacted by email. If so, be sure you have either on-line resources on your church website or websites you can refer people to.

The American Tract Society has an excellent collection of tracts that answer many spiritual questions. They are available at:
www.atstracts.org

Faith Resource links from my website, www.effectivechurchcom.com

This is part of a longer list on my website, www.effectivechurchcom.com, the links are live on this site and you can click directly to the resources. You can also copy them from the website into your website for easy seeker access.

Ten Reasons to Believe, https://discoveryseries.org/ten-reasons/
An excellent site to explore the Christian faith in detail. Contains a number of lists including: *Ten reasons to believe in life after death, Ten reasons to believe in Christ rather than religion, Ten reasons to believe in the Bible.*

Christian Research Institute, www.equip.org/
This is the website of the Christian Research Institute and Hank Hanegraff, the Bible Answer Man. There are answers to many questions and links to many resources on this site.

Who is Jesus? www.whoisjesus-really.com
Lots of questions answered here about Jesus.

Campus Crusade for Christ, www.cru.org/
Lots of information for those exploring the Christian life and for those who want to live it. The ministry has changed over the years with a new name and new look but still has solid resources.

Our Daily Bread, www.rbc.org/odb/odb.shtml
A wonderful daily devotional for both new and more mature Christians.

Stand to Reason, www.str.org
The tag line for this site filled with answers to challenges to the Christian faith is "Confidence for every Christian   Clear thinking for every challenge   Courage and grace for every encounter." That's a great summary of what's on the site. They also have excellent resources specifically for students.

Radio Bible Class Ministries, www.rbc.org/
There are a wealth of resources on this site for growing in your Christian life. There are Bible reading plans, articles on finding a church, answers to many questions people have about the Christian faith.

OnePlace.com, www.oneplace.com/
A very fun site and educational site. This site contains the links to many Christian radio stations. You can listen to your favorite radio preachers live here and can download messages.

In addition, many denominations have resources that are helpful to answer spiritual questions. Check out your denominational publishing houses for these resources and link to your denominational websites from your church website.

If you have other sites you think are useful for churches to know about and link to or that are helpful for visitors, please let me know. Email me at yvon@effectivechurchcom.com

Social Service Resources

Though you are a church and the spiritual welfare of people may be your primary concern, many times people will come to your church and will reach out on a connection card for answers to physical needs. In addition, though a primary need expressed may be spiritual, a tangible physical need may go along with it.

For example, a woman might write on her card, "My marriage is in trouble and I'm afraid, please, can I talk to someone?" If a pastoral call reveals severe abuse, the referral of a domestic violence program may be needed.

If someone writes: "I've been out of work for two months and things are getting tough." A pastoral call may reveal a need for referral to a food bank and utility payment assistance.

Jesus met many physical as well as spiritual needs and we should be prepared to do the same.

There are many situations like this and to help your pastoral care team respond, have in place the following resources with listings that include:

· contact information

· services provided

· costs or requirements for assistance

Often you don't have to put together this list yourself. Contact local governmental or social service groups—most cities already have these lists in place.

The list of suggested groups that follows are not exhaustive, but merely a start for what you might need. Your church location (rural or big city), the age groups you primarily reach (youth, young families, seniors), each of these groups will benefit from you being prepared with specialized resources.

Social Service Resources to include information about:

· Food banks

· Emergency housing

· Transportation services

· Crisis pregnancy

· Battered women shelters

· Child protective services

· Any specific needs or ministries for your church or community

· Mental health related resources

· Pastoral counseling referrals

· Christian counseling referrals

· Guidelines on when to refer to outside counseling

· Alcohol or drug 12-step, recovery and treatment programs, both church and secular ones

· Pornography addiction and counseling services

· Grief recovery

· Divorce recovery

· Additional resources unique to your community such as support for military families with members deployed overseas.

Test phone number, website addresses, and all contact information periodically to make sure it is current.

You do not want to disappoint a person in need by giving them a phone number that is no longer in service.

Be sure that you periodically test the phone numbers and make certain the information you give out is current.

It would be terribly disappointing to someone to receive a recommendation from your church and a referral for assistance only to get a message that the number is no longer in service. If you can give people needing help the specific name of a person who can help them that is even better. If you have a team of people who can go with them to the agency and who can follow up to make sure that people get the help needed, that is best of all.

More than any words we flash on a screen, your care of the less fortunate communicates the reality of Jesus in the life of your church.

Now that your resources are in place consider the triage model

You cannot and do not need to respond to every connection card at the same time or in the same way. You will get a wide variety of input on the cards ranging from a simple change of address notification to news of a church member involved in a severe accident, to a personal loss or tragedy, to a visitor request for more information, to a volunteer signing up for children's ministry. Obviously not every card has the same urgency regarding the response needed.

To balance church resources and the needs of people, the concept of triage might be helpful. The next chapter defines it and shows how it can provide a model for responding to the needs expressed on communication cards.

CHAPTER SIX

Triage, a model for responding to connection cards

It is critically important to respond to the connection cards received each Sunday, but as stated in the previous chapter, not every card needs the same timeliness or intensity of response, but how do you decide what needs what?

The concept of triage can help.

First, here is the history and definition of TRIAGE from Wikipedia, the online encyclopedia:

TRIAGE

The term [triage] comes from battlefield or natural disaster situations. When the wounded are brought in there are three categories in which the wounded are immediately placed:

Red / Immediate

They require immediate surgery or other lifesaving intervention, and have first priority for surgical teams or transport to advanced facilities; they "cannot wait" but are likely to survive with immediate treatment.

Yellow / Observation

Their condition is stable for the moment but requires watching by trained persons and frequent re-triage, will need hospital care (and would receive immediate priority care under "normal" circumstances).

Green / Wait (walking wounded)

They will require a doctor's care in several hours or days but not immediately, may wait for a number of hours or be told to go home and come back the next day (broken bones without compound fractures, many soft tissue injuries).

From http://en.wikipedia.org/wiki/Triage

How to apply triage to connection cards

Though you aren't dealing with actual battlefield situations, this model is useful in responding to the connection cards you will receive from those fighting spiritual battles each week. In an ideal world, your staff would be able to follow up immediately with every need; but our ministry worlds are often far from ideal.

Following are suggestions for how to apply the three levels of triage in how you respond to the people turning in connection cards:

RED: those needing immediate follow up or care

An immediate scan of the cards for people in severe crisis may be literally lifesaving.

Some people will be in severe crisis—some weeks perhaps no one will be, but sometimes you will have a person teetering on the edge of suicidal despair. Because of that, if at all possible, it is recommended that someone go through the cards immediately after they are collected. In some large and well-staffed churches, immediately upon receiving the cards paid staff immediately screen the cards, enter information into a database, email responses, make necessary pastoral calls, and schedule additional follow up, all on Sunday afternoon.

Many churches cannot do this, but if a pastoral team member (volunteer or paid) could make it their responsibility to go through the cards looking for people who are in the "Red" category and honestly may not make it through the week without a contact, that would be excellent.

Other churches are not able to do all the data entry on Sunday, but do have hospitality or visitation teams either call or email visitors or those with pastoral needs on Sunday afternoons. Again, in even the smallest church, a dedicated and committed volunteer could make it their ministry to do this on Sunday.

For many churches, Monday is the soonest that a staff member can get to the cards, but if at all possible, do make it a priority. Also, no matter what the time or day, sort the cards into the three levels and be sure as soon as possible someone responds to those in the RED category

YELLOW: those who have real needs, but not in the emergency category

Worth repeating: ALWAYS respond to volunteer responses within ONE WEEK of getting the connection card or you will send an extremely negative message and people will much less likely to respond to you when you ask for volunteers in the future.

These situations often require a judgment call as to whether they are in the RED or YELLOW category. Though these folks communicate specific needs, they are ones that can be answered in the span of perhaps a few days to a week after the church service. It would be best to come up with guidelines in your church to help you make decisions about which category to place various needs.

Also in this category, place those who are responding to any call or request for volunteers. **Volunteer requests should always be responded to within a week.** If people volunteer and you don't contact them, they may feel you don't care, or their offer to volunteer didn't matter and they may not volunteer in the future.

If you or the department asking for the volunteers will not be able to make personal contacts right away either a postcard or email could be sent out as soon as possible that says something like:

> *"Thanks so much for volunteering for (whatever the department is). We'll be calling, emailing you later this week to work out the specifics. Our church is greatly blessed with people like you!"*

In addition, be sure to follow up with the department that asked to have the volunteer request put on the connection card to make certain they followed up to contact the potential volunteer.

If a pattern emerges where follow up is not done for any variety of reasons, when that ministry leader asks to put out a call for volunteers into the bulletin or on the connection card in the future, gently ask and seek a commitment for follow-up. Remind the ministry leader that hurt, disappointment, and mistrust can result from a request for help that is not responded to when it is offered. If the pattern continues, it may be best to gently let the ministry leader know the church office can no longer post volunteer opportunities on the connection card for that particular ministry, if follow-up connections are not being made.

Sad, but true example

Don't get people excited about a program or ministry and ask for volunteers if you don't follow through.

You may have tried something, decided it was not worth the effort, and are on to the next church growth best-seller, but if you ask for people to be involved in something, they volunteer, and you drop the program without explanation or apology, the consequences to the people who volunteered may be considerable.

Though we are adults on the outside, most people have very tender hearts inside and will not repeatedly volunteer if their responses to help are ignored or mismanaged.

During one church service the pastor talked at great length about the importance of prayer, how he was building a prayer team, and wanted people to volunteer to be on it. He shared that he had just read a book on the importance of prayer in growing a church and that it moved him deeply. He said he realized his needs in this area and he emotionally pleaded for volunteers to join a team who would pray together with him about his burdens of ministry and needs of the church.

A long-time church attendee, a man who had been in the background and who had not volunteered in the church before, but who loved to pray, was deeply moved, and decided to volunteer. His wife usually filled out the connection card for the family, but this week he wanted to do it. A quiet man, for whom so many requests for church involvement in the past had seemed impossible, this was something he could do. He checked the box asking for volunteers for the pastor's prayer ministry and also wrote a personal note on the connection card about how much this would mean to him to be part of this. He turned in the card, feeling more hopeful about church involvement than he had ever felt before.

Each day, he would check his email and postal mail for a response. He frequently asked his wife if perhaps he had missed an email or phone message. Two months went by before his request received a response that turned out to be very different from what had been initially presented at the church.

The meeting was handled by a volunteer, who immediately said she couldn't continue to coordinate this and someone else would have to do it. The pastor briefly appeared and said the people would get monthly emails on prayer requests. No, they wouldn't actually be meeting with the pastor to pray.

A few more months went by. No follow-up emails. No acknowledgment to the people who volunteered. No pastoral prayer team continued.

Though still attending the church, it is doubtful the man will ever respond to a volunteer request from the pastor again.

There are so many reasons and most likely very valid ones why this happened—I can hear many pastors protesting that people must understand the demands on their time, the unexpected that comes up, and all the related reasons. All true, again all valid, but in spite of that:

Pastors, leaders, and teachers, please—*remember how important you are to your people.*

Leaders are in a key position both to heal and to hurt—remember that before you ask for a response from volunteers.

Remember you are in a position of great power to not only lead and teach, but to deeply hurt and disappoint. Remember that people put great faith and hope in what you say. If you ask for a response—no matter what, be sure you respond back to the people. Plan to do it; block out time for it; make it a priority or you may lose spiritual credibility and the hearts of your people.

Even more tragically, you will probably never be told how deeply your inaction hurt. And if you could not be trusted to respond to a request you initiated, how can you be trusted to respond to an emotional pain or spiritual question?

All of us in leadership have been guilty of this, I know I have been. We all need forgiveness for asking people to do things and then dropping the program or project without explanation. The advice I try to follow for those of us ready to try new things, to get people involved, to quickly charge into action before counting the cost, is that we slow down, pray, and work out a follow-up and involvement plan for people who will respond to our requests before we needlessly ask for help we won't ultimately use.

Information about ministries without a specific volunteer request

Every church is challenged with attracting and retaining volunteers. Before looking for some new or complex solution, review how you respond to simple, ongoing requests often on your connection card.

A subcategory of volunteer responses is where many church connection cards have a series of boxes that people can check for information about men's, women's, children's, music, etc. Or perhaps the card has a nonspecific statement, such as "If you would like to be part of any of these ministries, check the box beside it."

It is very important that if people check these boxes that they get a timely response. Sometimes in churches that information is not passed on in a timely manner to the ministry leaders, or a list of people who checked the ministry box gets lost in a staff member or volunteer's in box. Again, to not respond when someone has reached out and asked for information or an answer can have devastating consequences.

In both this instance and in the instance of someone volunteering, we never know how much personal courage it might have taken for a person to volunteer for something or ask for information about a ministry program. Perhaps they have never been involved in a church before, but feel they ought to do something; perhaps they were emotionally wounded in a another church, have been away a long time, but now feel they want to try some small volunteer task. Checking that box may have been a huge act of courage and hope. PLEASE do not disappoint by failing to respond in a timely manner. Below is a suggestion that will make responding much easier.

An easy way to response to these specific ministry requests

One way to solve this challenge for the checked boxes where people want information about a specific ministry, is for the church office to have on file basic information packets, brochures or forms that describe the ministry areas and then give information on who to contact for further information or how to become involved. The brochure could be sent out with a follow-up letter. An electronic version could be forwarded to an email address.

A personal contact is always best, but if a person gets for example, a cheery packet about the children's ministry with a note that "Miss Becky or one of her wonderful helpers will be calling you in the next week" it gives the staff person a bit more time to respond knowing that an initial contact has been made.

GREEN: the cards that are more administrative in nature; change of address, new email, etc.

Just because a visitor does not specifically state on their card that they are dying inside, does not mean they would not benefit from a timely, personal response.

You never know the lonely pain that might be behind the simple checking of a box, "new in town" or "first visit to the church."

If you take time to respond, you'll make a greater impression than the most astounding media Sunday service ever could.

Though this is the third level in the triage model, in many instances this is the action that takes place first as the response on cards are entered into a database or church management program. An immediate triage sort should have set aside those cards that needed action immediately; the remainder can be set aside and these fall into the "OK to enter later" group.

Though these cards may not require immediate pastoral action, it is very important that whoever does this be given a vision of the value of this ministry of recording. As stated earlier, the Bible records many instances of the value of careful records, the entire book of Numbers being one of the primary examples.

With probably the most important record being the one kept by the Lord, in the "Lamb's Book of Life," and it is not too much of a stretch to say that the first step in someone becoming a member of God's forever family is a record of their visit to the church that will then be followed up in a timely and caring manner.

If your church truly wants to stand out in our media-saturated, glitz, glamor and ultimately empty world, don't try to do it through more media, more noise, more flashing videos or slick promotional postcards. Try a personal phone call or email to every visitor, where someone actually has the time to interact and answer questions about the church and the Christian faith. If you do that, you will be unforgettable.

Paperwork often proceeds personal contact

With the value of this ministry in mind, the actual processing of the cards should be managed with the upmost care and prayer. They should be attended to in the most timely and efficient way possible.

After a brief pause to look at digital responses to connection cards, in the next chapter, we'll look at one of the best tools for handling this important information: Church Management Software.

Digital response options to connection cards
.............and what can be a big problem in conflicting expectations

We are in a transition time as I write this book, where a variety of digital forms of communication including email, texting, using Twitter or Facebook are the preferred methods of communication for many people. People expect to communicate to businesses, service providers, friends, every other entity or person they interact with via digital methods. At a minimum, if they send an email, they expect a response to their email.

The potential problem comes in because many senior pastors and staff in churches went to seminary (my husband among them) before computers, let alone email, was invented. Many of these pastors have and continue to oversee very successful churches. They may never or seldom use email personally and do not see a need for it. In addition, many up-front pastors, even if they are technologically skilled, are outgoing, active people and the idea of spending hours at the computer, thoughtfully answering email or responding to visitors via email is simply not something they are interested in doing. These pastors may or may not use a cell phone consistently. Even if they do use one (again, my husband as an example) they may only use it for voice communications, not texting or tweeting.

The challenges won't disappear

There will always be new technologies. How you handle issues today need to be wisely determined for how the technology that comes along in the future will be handled.

There will come a day when your iPhone will no longer be the latest and greatest tech toy and texting and tweeting will be outdated and passe.

But the need to seize new technologies for the sake of the gospel will never be outdated.

First of all, we need to realize that this is not simply an issue that will last until the baby-boomer pastors retire.

There will always be new technologies. There will always be people on the bleeding edge of the latest gadget just as there will always be those who neither care or are concerned and live just fine without them. On the extreme end there are those who see every new technology from television to the web as the devil's latest playground.

In addition to personal feelings, some churches have the money to experiment with every new tool that appears and others either do not have the money or have made a conscious decision to use their resources for other causes.

In the midst of these varied responses, all within the body of Christ, we must find a balance that respects the communication styles of our leaders while meeting the communication needs of our church communities and visitors. In an attempt to do that, following are a few practical suggestions on how to deal with email today. Substitute for email any technology causing you similar concerns in your church.

1. Have an honest discussion about what technology tools the staff is expected to use. Make sure everyone at the church is trained on the system your church has chosen to use for email and other forms of digital communication. Make it very clear who is expected to learn and use it.

2. Don't put a pastor's email address in the church bulletin, connection card, or web church directory if he or she is not going to answer their email. That is disappointing, deceptive, and rude. The pastor may not even realize his or her email is listed in these ways, never checks the email account set up for them by the helpful tech volunteer, and wonders why various people in the church are angry with him or her.

If someone else is assigned to answer the pastor's email, be honest about who is answering it. I do this for my husband. I am very clear when I do it and always say something like, "I shared your email with Pastor Paul. This is what he wanted me to share with you." I work very hard to communicate his thoughts and only those and frequently read an email to him before I send it to make certain it is what he wants to say. This process probably sounds old-fashioned (think secretary with dictation pad) and time-consuming. It is. Fortunately right now my husband does not get a lot of emails in his ministry. If this increased greatly I would have to get some help in doing it.

Respect is important for church leaders and to not be honest about technology skills or your lack thereof can be destructive to the respect and trust your people will have for you.

It would be unrealistic for me to think my husband will ever be greatly excited about answering his own emails and I don't know that he should. He is fantastic with people pastorally and in an up-front, personal way I could never be. I don't go on camp-outs or do the heavy-duty construction on mission trips that is easy for him. He doesn't do email or create websites. We support and work with each other from our respective skill areas.

Consider perhaps a Minister of Pastoral Technology. We have specialized pastors and volunteers in many areas, what about one who was not just involved with technology as in hardware and website upkeep, but an altogether different person who approached technology as a pastor? Perhaps you could hire someone who responded to the email the church received, who handled Twitter and Facebook and whatever other social media the church used; someone who perhaps conducted on-line meetings, counseling or training. Blogging could also be part of this person's responsibilities.

IMPORTANT CLARIFICATION: To repeat, I am not talking here about hiring an IT (Information Technology) person or someone who creates a website or who handles the networking, digital imaging and other technology jobs around the church, though that can be an important position. IT is a technical job; what I am suggesting is a pastoral one. Though the work could be combined, it often requires a very different skill set for each activity. I have found a person with a pastoral heart can often be taught functional tech skills, but sometimes a real geek (and I use the term with great love and admiration), someone who thinks in computer code and circuits, doesn't always have an interest or ability in the pastoral aspects of church social networking ministry.

Whatever you do be honest about it

I recently experienced the negative response you can have to a lack of honesty in this area, when I attended a conference by a pastor who had written a very helpful ministry book. I had the opportunity to ask him during the break how he thought his ideas worked in the current climate of email, social networks, etc.

He answered that he had no idea and that he "wasn't into that stuff."

I bought his book and in it the author (him, I assumed) talked about the various ways some of his ideas worked out in the current climate of email, social networks, etc. This was a completely different picture of the church's use of technology by not only the congregation but by the pastor, according to the book. Which version of the church's technology use was correct?

A unfortunate pattern from the past, transferred to the present

Since in the past I worked as a ghostwriter for a number of Christian organizations in Colorado Springs, I suspected what was going on.

As often happens in these situations, someone wrote his book for him, using his seminar notes (which was obvious from the similar structure of both). In addition to the basic seminar content the person who wrote the book understood the implications of technology and the need to be current and so he put in the information about technology.

Nothing so far is a problem. Similar to my illustration about doing the email for my husband, there are many instances in the church where the up-front person does not have the time or training to write a book. The ministry has a message that needs to be shared and often a ghostwriter, co-writer, whatever you want to call him or her is asked to write the book.

The information and application suggestions added to this book were all quite good, but here are the problems:

1. In the book, the speaker/author did not acknowledge his ghostwriter or the process used to create the book.

2. The ghostwriter apparently did not communicate to the author what he added and why it was important.

3. I do understand in the press of getting books done how this can happen, but it isn't honest and there is no reason not to be honest about this. Nobody can do everything; we need each other, but we shouldn't be phony about it, no matter what our place on the ministry team.

We can't all do everything and we should no more hide who does our technology than we would who cares for the children or teaches adult education classes.

The author and ghostwriter could have modeled the interactions of helping one another in technology and sadly they didn't. Don't let that happen in your church.

Tune up, expand your website

In addition to being honest about who is creating what, give your website a checkup before you begin to respond to people.

Many of your responses to visitors will be on paper, but often you will want to refer them to additional information on your website. You need to carefully and honestly answer the question, "Is your website ready for this?"

A huge problem that I've seen with many websites recently is that churches spend money to get a website designed or created by a national church website company. They spend lots of money on it because the church knows a website is important today and no one on the church staff feels confident to create the website.

The website is finished and often the home page looks great—beautifully laid out, lots of color, usually moving images and happy people grace the layout. However, there is often a problem in that if you click on anything you are often taken to a page that has a sentence or two, and often outdated or incomplete information. They are a bit like some of the old movie sets: a great facade, but behind it, no real structure.

People go to a church website for facts, all else is icing on cake, pleasant, but not essential

Why do you go to a website, any website? You go to it for information. Your structure has to be solid for people to trust you and your church. Be sure your church website has:

• Complete information about the people, ministries and programs

• Contact information for each ministry

• Times, dates, locations, links to mapping programs

• All information up-to-date

• Clear ways for people to contact you and a system in place that assures timely response.

There is much more on www.effectivechurchcom.com on creating and maintaining church websites, but for now, ask the Lord to help you see your website with the eyes of a visitor. Is all the information you need easily available and understandable? If not, be sure you make some changes before you refer people to it.

CHAPTER SEVEN

Church Management Software and Connection Cards

How do you organize all the wonderful information you collect every week with your connection cards?

How do you keep track of visitors and of your follow-up contacts with them?

Technology comes to the rescue of the increasing complexity and growing numbers churches work with today in the form of Church Management Software.

If you are already using a Church Management Software program

If you already are using a program you will want to be certain that your connection cards are designed with that program in mind. The kind of information you ask for and how you respond to people can be greatly influenced by the software program you use.

Be sure that the person who maintains the program and the people who input the data are consulted as you design the cards. Check with them to make sure that the layout of the cards makes data entry as easy as possible. For example, be sure you leave enough space for people to comfortably fill out information. If the area you have for the email address is too small and people have to tighten up their writing to fit it in; or if you have a slick surface that is hard to write on and then to read, you may miss vital information when it comes time to enter it into the database.

If you are looking for a Church Management software system

As I started working on this update, I found that the programs and companies I highlighted a few years ago have either gone out of business or have changed beyond recognition from what they were.

Because of that I deleted that section and the best advice I can give you is to get referrals from churches your size as to what works best for them.

Being in ministry means doing things for people

Regardless of the software you use, this is one of the most difficult parts of a connection card ministry and it's worth remembering the example Jesus gave us when he washed the disciples feet.

If we want to keep track of our visitors and the people in our congregation, we will most likely have to pick up the towel and water of church management programs and keep doing the foot-washing work of careful data entry. This work is often tedious and usually not fun, but an opportunity to serve as Jesus served.

CHAPTER EIGHT

More ideas on follow up of connection cards from visitors

It's a continuing challenge—when you get a large number of cards turned in it's easy to think your task is done. But it isn't.

You've got to triage and record everything. It's then easy to think that when you finish recording the work is done—but more challenges lie ahead!

No matter what system you use to record visitors, the ideas following will apply to any Church Management Software (CMS), because no matter what the ways of record keeping on the computer, you have to decide how to actually contact the people.

The CMS system can be challenging to learn and that can be deceptive, because it is easy to think that once you learn the system, you've got the task managed. But CMS is simply a tool to connect with people—success is defined by a actual, on-going connection with people and changed lives, not an efficiently running database.

To emphasize: *you* are in charge of any program that you purchase, no matter how effective it may seem, how efficient on the computer, how easy it is to enter and organize data, you are responsible for how your CMS touches people.

Ask the Lord to give you a tender heart to see into the needs and fears of visitors as you create your materials. Pray as you send things out that people will be in a receptive mood when they get your materials and that they will return and continue their spiritual journey with your church.

How to contact first-time visitors

No matter how technologically savvy we are today, still nothing beats an upbeat printed piece to connect with visitors.

After visiting a new church, some studies have shown the preferred way people want to be contacted is through the mail. Today email would also be a preference. Personal visitation may be considered an unwelcome intrusion. Follow-up phone calls can be perceived as just another form of annoying solicitation.

Some people like phone calls, others don't. If they work for you, fine, use them, but even if you make a phone call and connect that way, you might also want to send out something through the mail or email.

Only one member of the family may get a phone message, but everyone might read a letter or postcard. An attractive, welcoming personal letter or postcard also doesn't interrupt dinner and isn't threatening.

If your visitor has indicated that they would prefer being contacted via email, many of the ideas below still apply with a bit of modification for their electronic format.

Following are some ideas to make the follow-up letter or postcard more effective:

Don't send generic junk mail

People aren't stupid. We all receive computer generated junk mail with preprinted signatures. Don't insult your visitors by sending them the same sort of piece that any direct mail marketer does and expect them to think it was personally signed by the pastor. If a pastor does not have time to personally sign welcome notes, don't put his or her name on the communication piece. Instead, have the welcome piece come from someone on a visitor or welcoming team sign it. Being phony friendly is no way to win people to your church.

At the same time, if the pastor does not have time to sign visitor notes, I would challenge that pastor to do a bit of time evaluation. The results of that evaluation are between you and your Lord, but remember that Jesus, our chief shepherd and example, knows all of his sheep by name—if you can't do that, don't take credit for a personal contact you did not make by having your name preprinted.

Jesus, our chief shepherd and example, knows all of his sheep by name—if you can't do that don't take credit for a personal contact you did not make by having your name preprinted.

Visitors who have come to you are souls for whom Jesus died. Honor his sacrifice by responding to them as individuals, not just as an address added to the database.

This doesn't mean you must send a personal letter to every person from the pastor. You can still have a variety of planned responses, but with perhaps a handwritten P.S., or some added note, honestly added by the church administrative assistant or welcome team member to let people know a person looked at their card. For example, if they checked a box that they have preschool children, say something like:

> *PS - Isn't it great to have young children! We want you to know that our church loves kids!*

> *I've included information on our preschool Sunday School program. Our MOPS (Mothers of Preschoolers) and Mothers Morning Out can be a great lifesaver to busy moms and you don't have to be a church member to come. If you'd like more info please call Mary Smith at 555-5555.*

Be certain to respond immediately if a visitor asks to be contacted

Sad, but true:

A graduate student moved to a new town after a sad and painful divorce. She visited three churches and asked on her connection card that someone call her; she mentioned she was new in town and very lonely. None of the three called. One sent a generic letter that was obviously intended for families with young children. She never went back to any of these churches. How different her life might have been if she had received a note like this:

Desperate needs and loneliness are difficult to communicate by simply checking a box, but if someone checks that they would like someone to call them, be sure to do it as soon as possible.

If you don't the results can be personally and spiritually devastating.

> *PS - I read your note that you are new in town and newly divorced. I'm enclosing some information on some programs you might find helpful—our Divorce Recovery and our Singles Book and Movie Group. You don't have to be a member of our church or even come regularly to attend. I'm also passing your name on to our associate Single Adult Ministry Pastor. His name is John Smith and he will call in a few days to see how we might be helpful to you as you adjust to your new life in a new place. My prayers are with you.*

Remember not every visitor is local

Sad, but true:

A couple visited a church while on vacation. They were active, mature, tithing Christians looking at the community as a possible place to relocate. They visited a church, filled out the visitor card, and asked that more information about the church be sent to them. The church appeared to be very seeker friendly and loudly proclaimed in their publications and on banners in the church lobby that 'PEOPLE MATTER TO US!" It looked like a place they could serve and support.

After they got home they received a generic form letter from the church with a colored printed signature, obviously faked. In addition, the letter thanked them for visiting and hoped they would make the church their church home and come back each week to the church which was located in Florida. They crossed that church off their list. Why, you might wonder?

Here's why: whoever sent out the letter obviously didn't take the time to notice that the visiting couple lived in Kansas. They had to notice the address to send the letter—but didn't pay attention to it when they inserted the generic letter. All their information on the card and the note they added told the church they were visitors from out of state.

What do you suppose that couple felt about the church? Do you think they felt they actually mattered as individuals, no matter what the church banner proclaimed, since the church sent them a letter obviously intended for local people? Instead of being excited to move to the city and get involved in a caring, outreach-oriented church, they didn't feel they would go to that church and bring unchurched friends in the future, if the church could not be trusted to respond appropriately to an out-of-town address.

What a difference it would have made if the letter would have at least been a generic letter for out of town visitors and said something like this:

> "Thanks so much for visiting our church! We noticed that your address is out of town. We don't know if you were on vacation or are considering relocating to our community. If you were on vacation, we trust it was restful and we welcome you to consider our church your church home away from home whenever you are in the area.
>
> If you were visiting and considering relocating to our area, please email me at pastor@genericmail and I'll be happy to send you our church relocation package. It tells you a bit more about our community and our church. If we can help you in any way at this transition time in your life, please let us know."

Again, letters like this are extra work, you actually have to read a connection card and craft an individual response, but to do that shows you are a church where people matter in reality and not just in slogans.

In addition to connecting with unchurched people, how you respond to a visiting couple might cause you to lose out on potential, hard-working, tithing church members who may be moving to your city and looking for a church in which to give and serve.

Some folks fill out a connection card as a test to see what sort of a church you are.

If they are new in a community and looking for a church, they might be testing to see how you respond to visitors. If your response to them is less than friendly, they may decide not to attend your church because they would not want their unchurched friends to receive the same response.

Optional materials to include when responding to visitors

Successful direct mail pieces usually contain more than just a letter. You are already paying the postage, so be creative on what you also include, for example:

Church overview brochure

Try adding an upbeat, well-designed brochure that gives an overview of the various ministries of your church. One church did that and in addition included a color-coordinated refrigerator magnet (made from an inkjet-printed business-card attached to the peel-off refrigerator magnets you can get at office supply stores) that gave the times each of the various events took place each week. You could also do that for ministries that the visitors might have expressed an interest in.

People may not have any idea what they are looking for in a church and so did not check anything on the connection card. They may not have any idea what churches do and an informative brochure lets them know what is available.

In addition people will often file a brochure like this away in a drawer for future reference. They may not have a need for a grief-recovery workshop at present, but if a personal tragedy strikes, they may pull out the brochure and contact your church.

In addition, be sure your church specifically refers to your website where visitors can go for additional information about the church and to perhaps read the pastor's or other staff member's blogs, listen to teaching clips, or watch brief videos.

Brochures about your church can be full-color, detailed, and complex or they can be simple and conversational.

BOTH can work well--the most important thing is that the communication you send to people accurately reflects YOUR CHURCH, not a designers idea or a copy of what someone picked up at a church growth conference.

Be who YOU are and the Lord will bring the people to you for whom your church will be the best fit for their spiritual growth.

Include ministry-specific materials

Previously we talked about including specific ministry information if people checked a box asking for it and that is vitally important to do.

Sometimes people don't ask for specific information, but from the other information given to you on the connection card, you can send additional information that is helpful to them. For example if both a husband and wife put their names on the card, it would be a correct assumption that perhaps the man would appreciate hearing about the men's ministry at the church even if he did not check a box (or you had a simplified card that did not list ministry options) asking for it.

The card illustrated here, shows the kind of piece you could insert. One of the reasons that it is business card size is that a man could put this in his wallet to remind him of the ministry. Sending a lengthy brochure to a man probably isn't the most effective way to communicate.

If the people checking the card put their ages in the 55 and above range, if your card has a listing like that, the brochure below would be appropriate to include. Be creative in what you create for different age and interest groups, but the most important thing to remember is to carefully read over the cards, pray for wisdom on how to respond to individuals and send them additional materials specific to their needs.

These two cards illustrate another insert you could put into a visitor response letter. You can make similar cards/mini-brochures for any ministry in the church.

There are videos on how to create these on my website at www.effectivechurchcom.com

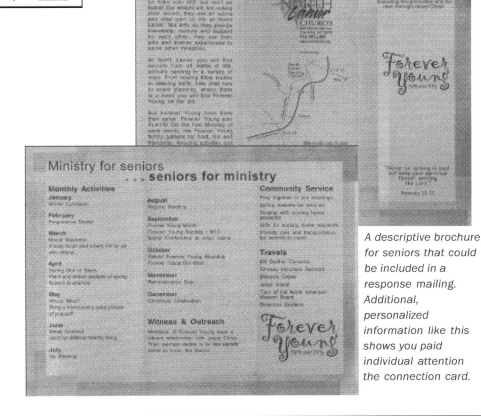

A descriptive brochure for seniors that could be included in a response mailing. Additional, personalized information like this shows you paid individual attention the connection card.

Invite them back for an more personal event or meal

You can modify the idea of this card to go along with whatever style works well for your church.

The design isn't nearly as important as the heart you put into it to reach out and connect with a newcomer.

To continue the connection started on Sunday, use your response communications to invite visitors back to an event where they can actually get to know people: a dessert, a coffee, a special time before or after the service, whatever seems to work well for your church.

The postcard to the left is very simple, but effective—it a makes a connection and gets people to an event where they can personally get to know other people in the church.

To be most effective, not only send a postcard, but also send an email and make a phone call to personally invite them. The phone call is the personal touch; the postcard gives them something to post on the refrigerator with the specific details when it is time to get in the car and attend.

Be sure when you host these events that the people from the church who are part of them have been trained well in how to interact with visitors. Nothing is worse than inviting a newcomer to an event where they are forced to sit alone and listen to someone up front talk about how wonderful and friendly the church is. No program is ever better than the people sitting right next to you.

Don't forget the value of tracts.

If you haven't looked at some of the current tracts you are in for a pleasant surprise. They are well-designed, contemporary, and very useful in sharing the gospel and encouraging Christian growth. Check out the web site at www.crossway.org.

There are many other ministries that produce tracts today in a large variety of styles and many languages. Because websites change so rapidly, the best thing to do is a Google search for current resources.

Tracts can be a powerful tool in the progress an individual makes towards coming to the Christian faith. If you have a good selection of tracts (and the Crossway site above has many, many of them) you can include tracts on specific holidays, on marriage and family issues, on questions people might have about the Christian faith.

A basic tract that summarizes the plan of salvation and how people can become a Christian is invaluable. In our post-Christian world today people will come to your church because a friend invited them or they were lonely or for many reasons, but they may have grown up knowing nothing about the Bible and Jesus. Don't assume anything when it comes to the eternal destiny of your guests. A clear gospel tract can introduce them to the Christian faith and help them understand where they are spiritually.

Whatever you do, ask the Lord to help you see individual faces and needy hearts as you prepare your follow-up communications for visitors. You are doing much more than sending out another direct mail project. You may touch lives in ways that can change hearts for eternity.

Yes, these sorts of personal responses take time, but if we really care about people, it has to be communicated by more than a generic form letter. Also, to really connect with people always takes more than one contact. Here is how it might work out in practice:

1. You send out an overall brochure about the church in your first mailing.

2. If you are going into fall, you might send out some information about men's football fellowship nights or information inviting them back to your alternative Halloween Harvest festival.

3. With Christmas coming, you might invite them to a night of carols and hot chocolate and enclose a little business card-size calendar for the coming year.

As always, tailor your mailings and gifts so they are appropriate both to the audience receiving them and making sure they represent well the church sending them out.

Little gifts can be fun and memorable

What you can include is limited only by your imagination. One church gave out free Starbuck's certificates, with a "Have a cup of coffee on us!" note attached. I'd remember a church fondly that did that.

A church in Canada took the idea of free coffee a bit further than the previous example and was highly successful. They included a certificate for two free lattes at the local Tim Horton's, (wonderful places similar to Starbucks, only they also serve soup). Along with the coupon was a note that said:

I LOVE this idea!

It shows you really do care about answering the questions of visitors to your church.

"Thanks so much for joining us at church on Sunday! As a thank you, we've enclosed a couple of free coupons for lattes at our local Tim Horton's. You can use them anytime you want, but we'd like to invite you to the local Tim Horton's on any Thursday afternoon from 2-4pm for Latte with the Pastor. If you come down then, you can ask any question you'd like about the Christian faith.

The folks who told me about this reported that it was wonderfully successful and though they had only been doing it for a short period of time, they had already started five seeker Bible studies from the latte with the pastor times.

Visitor packets, bags, mugs, etc.

Sometimes you want to do more than send a letter. Some churches either have a gift they give to visitors at a welcome center or that they respond with by taking a gift as they call on newcomers.

A church in Hersey, PA would take around to visitors a mug filled with Hersey

Kisses, that they called their "Mugs and Kisses" gift for visitors. It was perfect for the area and always received with a smile.

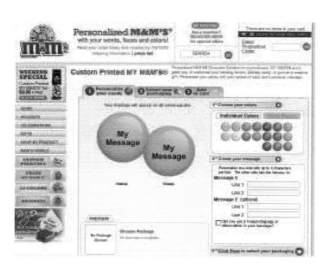

In addition to kisses, you can also get custom printed M&Ms. I imagine that munching on yummy little M&Ms that had the name of your church or some nice slogan on them, would be a bit of an incentive to return for some. If you are interested, here is the website for custom printed M&Ms: www.mymms.com

In the secular world, people sometimes refer to the free stuff they get at trade shows as "swag" and today lots of people really like the stuff. They keep it around and your business or service is always in front of them.

For mugs, pens and all sorts of other items you can use for initial and continuing contact with visitors and to use as a response to visitors, these folks are the best:

I'm torn about even mentioning doing something that adds more junk and stuff to our lives, but if a colorful mug or other item helps people think well of your church and brings them back—I imagine it is worth it.

As with everything, if you try using some of these kinds of products track cost and response.

Christian Tools of Affirmation
800-999-1874

www.ctainc.com—their main website

Not only will you find items that are useful for visitor follow-up, but they have all sorts of great holiday related items, volunteer appreciation and recognition items and lots of free, downloadable templates for children's and other ministries.

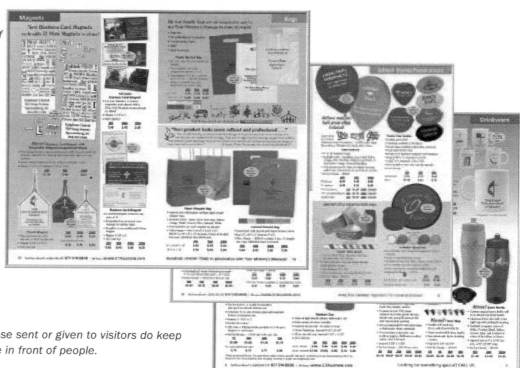

Little gifts like these sent or given to visitors do keep your church name in front of people.

CHAPTER NINE

Using connection cards for prayer requests

Praying for one another is a wonderful privilege of being part of the body of Christ. However, how a church collects and distributes prayer requests can become a complex challenge unless the church is very tiny. As a church grows, sometimes prayer requests, because of the sheer number of people asking for prayer, become little more than generic lists of names in the bulletin under the topics of: "Sick," "Out of Work," and often today, "Deployed overseas." Although churches who organize prayer requests in these ways are doing the best they know how, these systems are seldom satisfying to anyone. As one person in one of my seminars said to me, "My church won't pray for me unless I'm either sick or out of work and I need prayer in lots of other areas!"

Connection cards may provide a helpful option here. Again, if your church has a way of handling prayer requests that works well for you the following suggestions can be happily ignored. But if you would like to have more people more deeply involved in the prayer requests, the following procedure works well. I'm highly committed to this plan because from personal experience with both a large church and many small groups and adult education programs my husband and I have found this method to be quite successful. I'll first describe the procedure in the way we did it at a church of approximately 1,800 members. After that, I'll share how we modified it for use in small groups and adult Sunday School or adult education programs.

Prayer requests using church-wide connection cards for a large church:

Important caution: people who are regular attendees will know your procedure for sharing prayer requests, so you will be tempted to skip over explaining it.

Please remember that visitors who may also desperately need prayer, and they need to have a careful explanation so they know how to share their prayer request.

If you are getting almost no prayer requests from visitors, work on your presentation and track responses.

1. The procedure described earlier in the book was used to give people time to fill out the cards and the connection cards were collected with the offering and procedures similar to the ones described earlier were used to handle the cards. The procedure was modified with a special emphasis on getting prayer requests. People were told both when the cards were first mentioned and just before they were collected, "We really want to pray for you; we have a prayer team who will confidentially pray for you; please share your requests with us."

2. Cards that had a prayer request were photocopied and passed on to a person who specifically was responsible for handling the prayer requests. (One little practical note here: if you put the prayer requests on the same side of the connection card as the name, you don't have to photocopy both sides of the connection card. Samples of this are in the Gallery section.)

3. After that, the requests were separated into two sections; one, those that people had marked confidential and two, those which could be shared with the entire prayer team (more about the prayer team a bit later). The person selected to do this was a wise church office professional and she had the authority to place requests in the confidential stack, even if they were not marked in that way, if she felt they should be there.

4. The confidential list was typed up and passed on to the pastoral team.

An additional idea for prayer requests: some churches place the ones that can be publicly shared in a notebook in their prayer chapel or prayer room where people can come and pray for others.

You might also consider an online prayer request room that is password protected. You can easily do this with WordPress.

Because the prayer requests were more than just a list under categories, most prayer requests were about a paragraph in length. The person typing it up was told to type it up as the requests were written; they were not to edit them for grammar, spelling, etc. If the general list contained something inappropriate or embarrassing to be shared with the entire prayer team, (however that particular church defined it), it was put into the staff/confidential list.

5. The remainder of the list was typed up and passed on to the prayer team. The prayer team consisted of the people in the church who had volunteered to be on the prayer team. They had signed a confidentiality and ministry agreement wherein they promised to pray for the people on the list and to not gossip.

6. The prayer list was then either mailed or emailed out to the prayer team members. Please make both mail and email options available. It is an extra bother today, with the ease of email, to send materials out through postal mail, but some of your greatest prayer warriors may not have email. In addition, if you have elderly folks who receive the requests through regular mail, be sure to type them up using a generous size type (12 to 14 points depending on the typeface) so the requests are easier to read.

7. The end result: God was at work at this church, people were prayed for and they knew their prayer requests were taken seriously. At this church if you turned in a prayer request on Sunday, by Wednesday 500 people would be praying for you.

Prayer request procedure for an Adult Sunday School class, Bible Study, Small Group or any ministry

A prayer request Connection Card does not have to be fancy to make a tremendous impact on a Sunday School Class, small group, or House Church. It is a way for you to know what is in the hearts of your people and to pray for them. Templates for this and many other prayer request cards are available for ECC Members at: www.effectivechurchcom.com.

My husband and I have found using connection cards for prayer requests to be such a powerful ministry tool we use them in every ministry in which we are a part whether it is a small group, single adult ministry, or a Sunday morning adult education class. Here's the procedure:

1. People are given the cards or they are on tables as they come in.

2. At some time during the course of the meeting time, the cards are pointed out and people are asked to fill out their contact information and prayer requests.

3. Because we didn't take an offering at this class there were instructions to place the card upside down on their table; you could also ask them to place it in a basket or box as they leave, or someone goes around and pick them up.

4. If the group is very small or just starting, the leaders may be the only ones who look at the cards and pray for people.

5. As the group grows in size and length of time together, you can form a prayer team and after the procedure above, then distribute the prayer requests after screening for confidential ones.

6. In addition, as the group grows and gets more comfortable with sharing you might also add a section for "Praises" on the card.

Super important!

There is no better way to connect with people and grow a church or ministry than by using connection cards in this way.

I cannot emphasize enough what an important pastoral tool it can be to use connection cards in this way. If you are starting or planting a church, getting any small group started, or want to know what is on the hearts of your people, there is no better way than these cards. People will share things on the cards they might not ever say in person, often simply because there is not enough time for you, as the leader to talk to people individually the day or evening of the meeting.

By using the cards you know the concerns of your people, what is in their hearts, what are their concerns, needs, and worries. You have a way to person-ally follow up, pray for and connect with people.

Not every card you get will be positive—in one single adult group we had, one young man used the prayer card each week to point out everything we did wrong that week. But even that was a privilege to receive. It seemed like he simply needed to get his criticism recorded. Once he did that, he didn't feel the need to gossip about his concerns all week and we weren't blind-sided by a concern that we didn't know about that festered and surfaced later.

Examples of the power of email prayers

Technology has given us incredible ways to connect with prayer. Following are some true stories, examples of email prayer links from *Computers and Your Ministry*, a newsletter my ministry published previously.

Friends church links prayer and ministry

Positive and true stories:

First story: An evangelistic team is sent into the jungles of Mexico to preach the gospel. On the team is a person with a laptop computer connected to the internet. The evangelistic meeting begins.

Back home in the U.S. prayer groups gather at the time of the meeting in homes around computer terminals. The email connection is waiting. Back in Mexico the computer connects. The message comes: "We just gave the invitation for people to accept Jesus—everybody pray now!" People hundreds of miles apart battle for the salvation of souls and welcome new brothers and sisters into the kingdom of God.

Second story: A young woman opens the meeting house of the Friends church in her small farm community in Kansas. It's prayer meeting night and she doesn't know if anyone else will attend. She sits quietly for a time, but no one shows up. She goes over to the computer where she knows there is an on-line prayer meeting in progress. She joins them. A moment ago she was alone; now she's linked with friends who welcome her by name and together they spend the next hour praying together as their fingers quietly fly across the computer keys in prayer.

Commentary: Since using the computer in ways similar to the ones described above, one administrative pastor in a Friends church says, "The people in our region have grown so much closer. Not only are we able to share prayer requests so much more quickly, but we've gotten to know each other much better through email also."

Be creative in your ministry applications of the computer—it's a great tool for people connections.

Computer prayer line provides ministry to 81-year-old

Betty was 81-years-old and living alone on a farm in the country. She had serious heart trouble and her doctor told her he did not know how much longer her weak heart would last. Her hearing was poor. It had gotten so bad it was difficult even for her to talk on the phone and because of her failing health, her church attendance was rare. But when she heard about the on-line prayer network at her church that was starting, she wanted to be part of it.

The computer changed her life in ways she didn't expect. When she couldn't sleep, she'd turn the computer on, go back over the list of prayer requests and spend time praying over them. Though her inability to hear had caused her to become isolated, she could now communicate freely online. She could send messages and encouragements to the people she was praying for. They began writing back. Folks from the church she'd gotten to know better online started coming by the farmhouse to visit.

Betty then asked the pastor if she could become prayer coordinator for her area. He agreed and her prayer responsibilities increased as she helped set up and encourage other prayer teams.

On a recent visitor to her doctor, after her examination the doctor asked, "Betty, are you taking something I don't know about?"

"No doctor," was her quiet reply.

"Well, I can't explain it," he said, shaking his head. "I don't know what has happened, but your heart is healthy."

Commentary: The unspoken hero of the story above is the pastor and some of his friends who found a computer, gave it to Betty, taught her how to use it and remained in touch through email to encourage her and answer questions. It wasn't an easy learning time for Betty or her teachers and it took lots of time, but what a great contemporary application it was of the command to "remember the widows in their distress, "(James 1:27).

Prayer ministries on-line are a fantastic area of ministry for senior folks and those who are physically shut-in. If other members of the body of Christ will help them to get set up and train them, they can have active, involved and life-changing ministries.

The starting point for many similar on-line prayer ministries can be through your connection cards.

Production

By now I trust you are convinced of the need to be committed to a careful and ongoing ministry of communication cards if you want to connect with visitors, grow your church in numbers, stay connected to your people, and help them grow in Christian maturity.

Now let's get practical

This section will help you produce the cards them selves by giving you:

· Overall practical production tips on creating communication cards.

· An example of how to create a Privacy Statement on your connection cards that may be useful.

· Lots of examples of different kinds of connection cards with commentary on what works well on them and what might be changed.

· A suggestion on software to use in creating your connection cards.

· A suggestion on hardware that works well to create connection cards.

CHAPTER TEN

Practical production tips to help you create connection cards

By now you have the vision, people and procedures in place for creating connection cards. Now, let's get practical.

The design of your connection cards

There are a few basics to remember when creating communication cards:

· This is not something people will keep; they will turn it in, therefore, it is not the place to print your church website, address, or phone number.

· It is a tool communication; you aren't creating it to win a design contest.

· It needs to be read and filled out from a distance—on your lap as opposed to a desk.

· The type needs to be large, simple and clear. No script or fancy type.

· You want to make certain that you have enough room between the lines to write comfortably. Be sure to physically test that before you finalize your design.

Tips to remember about the physical construction of the connection cards

A digital duplicator will produce connection cards inexpensively, on 60# to 110# cardstock that are easy to write on.

Copiers produce beautiful bulletins, but don't work as well for connection cards.

· For the reasons given earlier, it is best if they are printed on card stock, on a separate piece rather than a tear-off portion of the church bulletin.

· Be sure they are printed on matte, not glossy cardstock.

· Be sure you write on the cardstock with the pew pens or pencils to make sure they write on the cardstock you have chosen.

· Be sure the design and printing method you use allows you to write on the communication cards.

There will be more about this last point in the next chapter, where I will make a specific recommendation, but sadly from my experience, I have seen too many connection cards that were either printed on slick, glossy paper or were designed with a toner-based image in the background that made them impossible to write on.

It isn't easy to remember these things

As you read over the tips above, you might think, "Oh, these are so obvious." But they aren't. I cannot begin to recount the many times I have had someone come up to me in my seminars who obviously, genuinely cared about reaching people, who had tried their best to create a connection card, but then no matter how good it looked, no one would fill them out. I especially remember one example, that was literally too beautiful—the next page tells the story.

The case of the too beautiful setting of a connection card

True story here (and I was given the samples and permission to share):

When the young man showed me his church bulletin and said that no matter what they did, nobody was turning in the connection cards, I carefully looked at what he gave me.

His church bulletin was a beautiful piece of artwork. Each week he created an original piece of art for the cover. The bulletin itself was a saddle-stitched bound booklet. The cover artwork pieces were wonderful; people loved them, collected them, and looked forward to getting them each week. After looking at the bulletin, as gently as I was able, I said, "You really don't know why nobody is turning in the connection card?"

"No." He said, sadly and honestly.

"Look" I said, as I held up the bulletin. The connection card was printed on the back of the cover of the beautiful artwork he created each week.

To fill out the connection information, you would have to tear the cover off the booklet. Then you could try to write on it!—Which

Each week the very talented communications director of this church would create a beautiful piece of artwork for the professionally printed and lengthy booklet that served as both a bulletin and church newsletter.

The only problem was that the connection piece was printed on the back side of the cover, which people liked to keep.

The problem is easily solved by printing a separate connection card on card stock and inserting it into the booklet.

Name: _____
Address: _____
City: _____
State: _____ ZIP: _____
Home Phone: ( ) _____
Work Phone: ( ) _____

I am:
○ A first-time guest
○ New to the area
○ A regular attendee
○ A member
○ Interested in receiving *The Outlook* newspaper
○ Interested in obtaining offering envelopes
○ Interested in volunteering

I would like information on:
○ A relationship with Jesus Christ
○ Understanding the Bible
○ Baptism
○ Church membership
○ Southeast's beliefs

I am interested in programs for:
○ Nursery ○ Ages 36-56
○ Preschool ○ Ages 57+
○ Grade(s) _____ ○ Singles
○ Ages 18-21 ○ College Age
○ Ages 22-35

I would like to be contacted by:
○ CARE Ministry *(care and encouragement to people in crisis)*
○ Children's Ministries
○ Choir and/or Orchestra
○ College Age Ministries
○ Country Lake Christian Retreat (Indiana)
○ Credit Counseling Ministry
○ Disability Ministry or Deaf Outreach
○ Facilities: Set-up, maintenance, and cleaning
○ Guest Services Ministry
○ Health Ministry
○ Food Service
○ Leadership Conference
○ Men's Ministry
○ Missions and Outreach Ministry
○ *The Outlook* Newspaper
○ Recreation Ministry
○ Restorative Justice
○ Singles Ministry
○ Single Parent Ministry
○ Small Group Services
○ Student Ministry
○ Support/Recovery Ministry
○ Visitation Ministries
○ Women's Ministries

If you have a prayer request, change of address, or want to send a message to a minister, please respond below: _____

_____

Welcome, Guests!

We are glad you chose to worship with us today.

Please stop by our Welcome Center, in the middle of the Atrium, for a map of the facility, as well as information on programs, classes, and other events offered at Southeast.

We invite all our guests, whether visiting Southeast for the first time or for several weeks, to join us for a Guest Reception held immediately after the service in the Fireside Room, which is located at the east end of the Atrium. Our ministers would love to meet you and answer any questions you may have about Southeast.

• As our guests, please do not feel obligated to participate in the offering. Instead, we hope that we are able to give something to you.

• Our communion service is open to all believers who have put their trust in Jesus Christ. Before the bread and juice are passed, the worship leader will give instructions as to how to partake of the communion.

FOR THOSE WITH CHILDREN: Our nursery and children's programs offer a warm, caring, and fun atmosphere, and they are well supervised. *Your child will be much happier with our well-trained caregivers than in the worship service.* Those seated around you will appreciate your thoughtfulness. The children's check-in area is located at the Registration Counter in the Atrium. Cry rooms are also available. Our ushers are here to serve you with any of these needs.

• To request more information on the Christian life or church membership, please complete the form to the left, tear it out, and place it in the offering plate as it is passed, or give it to one of our ushers at the conclusion of the service.

was almost impossible because it was printed on high gloss paper. After having destroyed the booklet, you would then turn it in. By doing that you would be giving away the beautiful picture.

He sighed.

I suggested that he simply take what he had on his connection form, print it on lightweight card stock and insert it into the booklet. That way people could fill out the cards, the church would get the necessary information, folks could keep the beautiful picture, the booklet wouldn't be torn apart, and hopefully everybody would be happy.

Does this mean we should do an ugly bulletin so folks will want to get rid of it?

Not at all—simply take a little time to think through the physical construction of the materials you hand out and don't let anything get in the way of making it easy for people to respond to you.

Below is an example of a church that also had a beautiful piece of artwork on it's cover. They printed their bulletin on matte paper which went well with the style of the artwork and their connection piece was a totally separate part of bulletin. Though I still prefer a detached, separate piece, this worked well.

Both sides of this bulletin are reproduced in the Gallery Section.

Guidelines for the style of your connection card

Like everything else that you create in the communications ministry of your church, your connection cards should look like your church.

Once basic format and construction details are taken care of, the most important thing is that when people see the card, that it looks like it comes from the same church that gave them the bulletin or whose website they looked at.

Looking the same includes things like being consistent in your use of colors, logos, etc., but it goes beyond that in that your materials should have the same style and feel. If you are a small country church, you might look one way, if you are a large, denominational city church another, if you live here in S. California like I do, probably a different look than folks who attend a church in downtown Boston.

Below are a few examples from different churches, one isn't any "better" than another; they all have been useful in their respective churches. Larger samples and in some cases the second side are in the following Gallery of examples.

*There are many styles and designs that work for communication cards—the most important design consideration is that it reflect **your** church.*

CHAPTER ELEVEN

Gallery of connection card examples

New and additional examples of connection cards will be added periodically to the website:
www.effectivechurchcom.com

Check the site out frequently for new materials to make your outreach effective.

There are a variety of connection cards in the following gallery reprinted to give you ideas for creating your own. The samples came from people who have taken my seminars and who shared their church communications with me along with permission for me to use them for teaching purposes. I thank them for sharing with me.

I included a number of samples of cards I have used in our ministries with Single Adults. They aren't the most exciting examples of graphic arts design, but they all worked extremely well in growing our groups (from 6 people up to 300 in a church of 1,800) and even more importantly, in groups of every size, we have stayed connected on a weekly basis with the needs and concerns of the group members, through the use of these cards. They are battle-tested.

Each page of samples has comments that may be useful to you—maybe one will inspire you or give you an idea that will cause you to modify something that isn't working.

The ones that I believe are most successful in getting people to fill them out and for the staff to follow up on are fairly simple because no matter how big or fancy your church, remember that the connection card is the doorway and often the first connection to your church. We don't want to make the entry to our church a confusion of many doors to enter as I fear might happen with some of the cards that have long lists of ministries and volunteer jobs.

Try different things and test to see what works best for you

I know what works for our ministries, but you are in charge of the spiritual welfare of your people and the growth of your church. No one knows better than you what will appeal to or work with your people.

Because the response can vary, test different kinds of connection cards—try a separate card if you have always used a tear-off, try ones with less or more information required. Track the responses and make decisions based on the results.

Send me your samples and continue the sharing

I'd like to put out a larger gallery of samples on future CDs on this topic and would love to have your samples—we all learn best from each other!

If you would like to be part of that, please send me a PDF (or you can send a MS Publisher or MS Word file) to yvon@effectivechurchcom.com with permission to use them. Include any thoughts, comments, or tips you might have.

I thank you in advance for your kindness.

Connection Cards for Single Adult Ministry—*that can be modified for any church, small group, adult education class or ministry*

In working with Single Adult Ministry for many years, my husband and I have found Connection Cards to be of immeasurable value. We've used them to grow our group and most importantly in many ways, to get to know what was on the hearts of our people, to pray for, and pastor them.

I've done up lots of cards and the following ones are representative of many done up in many situations.

Sometimes simple works best. We used this very simple card for a prayer team that prayed for our single's group on Sundays after class.

After Sunday, my husband, a bi-vocational pastor who works as a handyman, would literally carry the cards with him wherever he went and pray for his people as he worked.

For another Single Adult ministry we did, I made up this card and added the request for information so I could use it for visitors and database entry.

We worked very hard to get everyone to fill one out and always got a 70-100% response. We always knew what was on the hearts of our people through these cards.

PRODUCTION NOTE: for both of these and all the ones like them I use the Postcard template in MS Publisher.

Modify as you go to try various information gathering methods and ministry options

I decided I wanted to collect people's birthdays, so I decided to try doing the cards like this instead of the smaller squares on the previous page. The group was growing, we were going to add a prayer team, so I also added the option of being able to have the prayer request just go to my husband and myself.

I learned from that trial that it isn't good to try to introduce a prayer team after you as the leaders have been the primary prayers from the start. Everybody just kept checking the private box.

People also (we work with some older singles) got a bit tense about the birthday entry. Also, I realized I got less out of a piece of card stock and that seemed to add up.

It didn't take long for me to go to back to the more simple 4- on- a- page as the previous examples showed.

We use a variation of that simple 4- on- a- page layout for every small group, Sunday school class, whatever we do as a way connect with people, get to know and pray for them.

Welcome to The Journey!
Name:
Address:
Phone:
Email:
Birthday(month & day):

How can we pray for you this week?
____ check here to if only to Paul & Yvon

Welcome to The Journey!
Name:
Address:
Phone:
Email:
Birthday(month & day):

How can we pray for you this week?
____ check here to if only to Paul & Yvon

Welcome to The Journey!
Name:
Address:
Phone:
Email:
Birthday(month & day):

How can we pray for you this week?
____ check here to if only to Paul & Yvon

Focus Singles @VMC Communication Card

name_____ date_____

address_____

city_____ state_____ zip_____

home phone_____ work phone_____

email_____

check here if address, phone or email change ☐

your birthday_____ (MONTH & DAY ONLY IS OK)

kids and ages_____

please check one: single☐ divorced☐ separated☐ widowed☐

Are you a member or regular attendee of VMC? yes☐ no☐

Any church and if so, which one?_____

Questions, comments, prayer requests or praises_____

_____

_____

_____

_____

Confidential prayer request for Pastor Paul only ☐

Today I decided to trust Jesus as Savior☐

I would like to know more about what it means to be a Christian☐

I'd like to be part of the prayer team☐ (be sure we have your address and email above)

Privacy statement and what will happen to this information: any information given on this sheet is confidential and will be shared only with the Singles Pastor, Single Adult Leadership Team, Prayer team, and appropriate church staff. It will not be used in any way for commercial purposes. This information is to be used to inform, pastor, and pray for singles. After collection each Sunday the cards will be given to the Singles Pastor, they will then be given to the Singles secretary for entry into the attendance and information data base. Prayer requests or comments that are marked confidential will be kept by Pastor Paul only, all other requests for the prayer team will be reproduced and distributed to the prayer team. Non-confidential comments will be passed on to the leadership team. If you want to be removed from the mailing list, contact Pastor Paul 805-642-2332.

Sometimes your production or the secretarial service available helps determine your design.

For a time we worked at a large church where we had a secretary and larger than usual printing budget—so I got detailed on the info I needed to collect and more extravagant on paper use. The church decided to do away with the program in a few months, but the additional information was very useful for the time we had a way to record it.

forgetting the past we press ahead

FOCUS SINGLES CONNECT CARD

Today's date_____

Your Name_____
O Male   O Female
If this is your first time, or if you have a change of information,
please fill in the following

Address_____
City, State, Zip_____
Phone_____
Email_____
Birthday (month and day only is OK)_____

Please check one:
O single   O separated   O divorced   O widowed

Please check one:
   O First time guest of_____
   O Regular attendee
   O Member of VMC
   O Member of church_____

Kids & ages_____

Prayer requests, answers to prayer, comments or other information:

_____
_____
_____
_____
_____
_____

O Today I decided to trust Jesus as Savior for the first time.
O I would like to know what it means to become a Christian.
O Confidential prayer request for Pastor Paul only.
Other prayer requests are shared with the Prayer Team only.

forgetting the past we press ahead

FOCUS SINGLES

I used this card before I decided I needed to have the Privacy Statement on the bottom of the previous page. I liked how this looked probably the best of all the ones I did for Singles.

The Count me in Card below is a modified connection card that worked great as a way to recruit volunteers.

Count me In! Card

____ I want to help the FOCUS Single Adult ministry develop a community that will reach Single Adults for Jesus Christ and help all of us grow to maturity in Him.

I can help in these ways:
____ I will pray for the group, whatever I think of.

____ I want to be part of the prayer team. I understand this means I will get prayer requests either sent or emailed to me every week. I will keep the requests confidential, but I will pray for the people and their requests. Each week Yvon & Paul will have specific requests I will pray for. ***we really NEED this, please consider signing up!

I would like to volunteer to help in these ways:
____ Setup on Sunday Morning. Be here as close to 10:30 as possible for a very quick rearrange and setup.

____ Serve as a Greeter or Helper for new people to help get out name tags, work the book table, introduce new people, whatever I can do.

____ Other ways: you tell us what you want to do. Do you have a skill? Want to host an event? Whatever I've thought of? Do you like to help at events? Just let us know. Or are you just available? Write your ideas below:

_____
_____
_____
_____
_____

Contact information: PLEASE PRINT CLEARLY—Thanks!
NAME_____
Street address_____
City, State, Zip_____
home phone_____
work phone (if OK to call at work)_____
email_____
Thank you so much for whatever you volunteered to do. We need everyone, but most of all we need PRAYER! Ask God daily to grow us all in our Christian lives and to give us the vision to how we can bring other singles into a growing relationship with Jesus.
This world will not last long—all that really matters is who we take to heaven with us.

Uses of a Privacy Guideline Statements in connection cards

People have asked in my seminars how and why I used the privacy statement in the previous example. Here is how it came about:

We were working with a Single Adult Group that was active in outreach and I observed how some hesitated when they first confronted our connection cards. I realized that we were asking total strangers to the group to give us private, detailed information and that might be a bit scary. I wanted to assure them it would be private and only used for the church group. I came up with several Privacy Guideline Statements that I used on cards like the example on this page.

People expect statements like this on any website they give information to; I thought that the church should do no less if we want credibility and trust with our target audience. We don't have to make a big deal out of it; I printed it on the cards, on the bottom is pretty small type, but for those who cared, it was there.

Below is the text, slightly modified from the one actually on the card illustrated. You are free to copy, modify and use any version of it if you would like.

Text on Privacy statement:

Focus Singles @VMC Communication Card

name _____ date _____

address _____

city _____ state _____ zip _____

home phone _____ work phone _____

email _____

check here if address, phone or email change ☐

your birthday _____ (MONTH & DAY ONLY IS OK)

kids and ages _____

please check one: single☐   divorced☐   separated☐   widowed☐

Are you a member or regular attendee of VMC? yes☐ no☐

Any church and if so, which one? _____

Questions, comments, prayer requests or praises _____

_____
_____
_____
_____
_____

Confidential prayer request for Pastor Paul only ☐

Today I decided to trust Jesus as Savior☐

I would like to know more about what it means to be a Christian☐

I'd like to be part of the prayer team☐ (be sure we have your address and email above)

Privacy statement and what will happen to this information: any information given on this sheet is confidential and will be shared only with the Singles Pastor, Single Adult Leadership Team, Prayer team, and appropriate church staff. It will not be used in any way for commercial purposes. This information is to be used to inform, pastor, and pray for singles. After collection each Sunday the cards will be given to the Singles Pastor, they will then be given to the Singles secretary for entry into the attendance and information data base. Prayer requests or comments that are marked confidential will be kept by Pastor Paul only, all other requests for the prayer team will be reproduced and distributed to the prayer team. Non-confidential comments will be passed on to the leadership team. If you want to be removed from the mailing list, contact Pastor Paul 805-642-2332.

Privacy statement and what will happen to this information: any information given on this card is confidential and will be shared only with the Singles' Pastor, the Single Adult Leadership Team, Prayer Team and appropriate church staff. It will not be used in any way for commercial purposes. This information is to be used to inform, pastor, and pray for singles. After collecting the cards each Sunday the cards will be given to the Singles' Pastor, they will then be given to the Singles' secretary for entry into the attendance and information data base. Prayer requests or comments that are marked confidential will be kept by Pastor Paul and Yvon only. All other requests for the prayer team will be reproduced and distributed to the prayer team. Non-confidential comments will be passed on to the leadership team. If you want to be removed from the mailing list for any time for any reason please contact Yvon Prehn at 555-555-5555 or email yvonprehn@aol.com.

Using 6-8 point type (Arial Narrow works well), and 6-8 pt. leading or very narrow line spacing , this statement fits well on the bottom of a connection card.

Following are additional examples of a variety of connection cards from a variety of churches

There is no perfect way to design connection cards, but the following ones might give you ideas.

Name	Date
Address/City/State/Zip Code	
Phone	E-mail
I came as a friend of	
Children/Age	

HOPE CHURCH

COMMUNICATION CARD

Status	Age Group	Today I Am	Please check one
☐ Junior High	☐ 12-17	☐ Already committed my life to Christ	☐ First time guest
☐ Senior High	☐ 18-30		☐ Returning guest
☐ Single	☐ 31-39	☐ Believing in Christ for the first time	☐ Regular attender
☐ Married	☐ 40-55		☐ Member
☐ Single Parent	☐ 56-65	☐ Considering Christ	
☐ Widow/Widower	☐ 66+	☐ Dedicating my life again	

Prayer Requests/Questions/Praises/Comments _____

I would like more information on:		Sign Me Up For	I would like to speak with
☐ Becoming a Christian	☐ Sunday School Classes	☐ Newcomer Luncheon	*(write in name)*
☐ Baptism	☐ Children's Ministry		Pastor _____
☐ Baby Dedication	☐ Kid's Promiseland	☐ HOPE 101	
☐ Becoming a Member	☐ Vacation Bible School	☐ Baptism Class	_____
☐ Hope Church Values & Beliefs	☐ Student Ministry	☐ Other	
☐ The Christian and Missionary Alliance	☐ Senior's Ministry	_____	_____
☐ Counseling	☐ Cells/Small Groups		
☐ Financial Counseling	☐ Cell Leaders Training		_____
☐ Men's Basketball	☐ _____		

I think this is a beautiful and well-designed card, one that would work well in almost any church.

The only tiny, change I might make on this (and it comes from practical experience) is that I would have people repeat their name on the second side with the prayer requests and other information. The reason for this is that often in churches the prayer request cards are photocopied. If that is the case, someone has to put the name of person on side with the prayer requests. Even if they are being typed in, though you can turn the card over, having people write it is easier.

A mail-in connection card

This is a novel approach, but the lady who shared it with me said it worked well. After the missions conference instead of taking up the mission commitment cards there, they asked people to take them home, pray about their response and then mail it back to the church.

This honors the decision-making process and since the church already has the basic information about the people attending the church, there is not the same pressure to make the commitments. The goal is that the people who take the time to pray, response and mail back in the card will also carry out their commitment to pray and support missions.

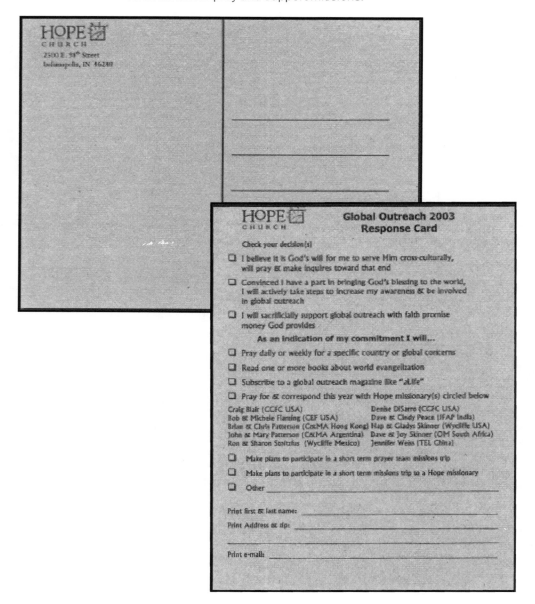

Welcome!

We'd like to get to know you better! Please complete this slip and place it in an offering basket. Thank you!

Name

Address

City/State/Zip

Home Phone ☐ TDD

Day Phone (if other) ☐ TDD

For our visitors...
☐ I am visiting New Hope for the first time.
☐ I am looking for a home church.
☐ I currently attend another church.
☐ I am visiting from out-of-town.

For our regular attendees...
☐ I would like information on becoming a member of New Hope.

I am a new believer in Jesus Christ...
☐ Please help me take the next steps.

Subscribe to the Ho'okele, New Hope's monthly newsletter...
☐ Please add me to your mailing list.
☐ I am receiving multiple copies, please delete this address from your list.

I would like to speak with someone about:
☐ Joining a Small Group.
☐ Becoming a Christian.
☐ Becoming a member of New Hope.

Prayer counselors are available to pray with you at the YES! table between services.

Prayer requests:

Praise reports:

Your name

Very nice clean, clear card.

My only concern would be that HUGE list of options people can check. If the church office really has the materials and can follow up on all the requests in a timely manner--good for them!

If the requests for all these areas cannot be completed within a week a much more manageable list would be my recommendation. Remember, it is better not to ask people for a response than to ask, have them respond, and then for the church to be too busy to connect with them.

I would like to volunteer my time serving in the following ministry:

☐ Adoption	☐ Levites (Set up/Take down)
☐ Baptism	☐ Lighting
☐ Bookstore	☐ Mechanics
☐ Children's	☐ Men's
☐ Choir	☐ Mercy Ministries
☐ Comm Servants	☐ Missions
☐ Conferencing	☐ Office Ministry
☐ Cooking	☐ Pac Rim Bible Institute
☐ Couples	☐ Parking
☐ Dance	☐ Photography
☐ Database	☐ Prayer
☐ Deaf	☐ Prison
☐ Drama/Programming	☐ Rebuilders (12 Step/
☐ Experiencing God	Support Groups)
☐ Gen-X (18 - 32)	☐ Research Ministry
☐ Greeters	☐ Singles (Crossroads 33+)
☐ Hawaiian Music	☐ Small Groups
☐ High School (Pureheart)	☐ Sound
☐ Ho'okele (Publications)	☐ Sports Ministries
☐ Hospital	☐ Tape Ministry
☐ Hospitality	☐ Ushers
☐ Japanese	☐ Video/Multimedia
☐ Junior High (TNG)	☐ Web Ministry
☐ Karaoke	☐ Women's
☐ L.E.A.D.	☐ Youth Choir

Name

Phone (Home)

(Work)

Best time to be reached:

Refer to the ministry list in this month's Ho'okele newsletter or visit the Small Groups table for a complete listing.

Hospital visitation requested.

Please visit:

Hospital and room #

Condition

Relationship

Phone number to arrange visitation:

Sample for a tear off

Though I do recommend a piece of card stock as a connection card, many churches get their bulletin shells printed ahead with the connection form as part of the shell.

One way to get more people to respond to this is for the pastor leader to say something like, "Let's all tear off our connection cards together and take time to fill them out now." That way a visitor isn't the only one in a row loudly tearing off paper.

How Are We Doing?

The Staff and Leadership of First Alliance are interested in how we can better serve you. Please feel free to offer us feedback, make suggestions, or ask any questions that you may have. If you desire a response, please include your name and address (on reverse side).

Prayer Requests/ Encouraging Words

Alpha

Thursday
6:00 p.m. in the Lower Auditorium, includes dinner.

Come explore the Christian faith in a relaxed, non-threatening manner.

Newcomers welcome!
To register, call 258-8288

Next Weekend at First

September 29/30
Saturday evening: 6:30 p.m.
Sunday morning: 9:00 & 11:00

History Makers
DO LIFE BY THE BOOK

Pastor Terry Young

Communion Service -- worshipping together around the Lord's Table

Sunday Evening, 6:00 p.m.
Prayer at the Cross

Chapel Hour
... begins the fall schedule on Sunday, October 14 at 6 p.m.

Guest speaker:
Rev. Bill Putnam of Polson, Montana

NOW! Contact Muriel (251-7582) or the MAC office (640-1053).

Tool Team ... offers assistance to single moms, seniors, etc. in accomplishing some simple household tasks. Volunteers are needed. Call Doug (242-4789) or Dave (256-1995).

Ushers (those serving now and those interested in serving) — you're invited to an informational meeting about ushering on Sun., Sept. 23 at 5 p.m. in Rm 9. Let's be ready to welcome and assist everyone who is going to join God's family and the First Alliance family this year.

Billets needed ... for delegates from across Canada who will be attending the College of Prayer at First Alliance ... Georgina (278-9499)

... wondered ... if God ... dance experience? ... ortunity to join a worship ... at First. We're looking ... en/women in dance and ... or more information, call ... 686-1749).

... as a part of the ... Growth on Oct. 13, ... fundamentals of ... offered. To help ... for the workshop, an ... will be held at the ... Oct. 1 at 7:30 p.m. ... the Information Desk to ... session ..

Church

Action Card
Thanks for being with us today. Please use this tear-off portion to pass on info to us, or request info from us. It can be placed in the offering plate or left at the Info Desk.
☐ New Attender ☐ Visitor
☐ Regular Attender
Age/Family Make Up:
☐ Preschool ☐ Grade School
☐ Jr High ☐ Sr High
☐ 18-28 ☐ 29-39 ☐ 40-50
☐ 51-64 ☐ 65 Plus

Tell me about these programs:
Children/Youth Activities
☐ Preschool (Birth - ECS)
☐ Grade School
☐ Jr High ☐ Sr High
Young Adult Activities
☐ Single ☐ Married
Adult Activities
☐ Women ☐ Men
☐ Seniors

I would like information on:
☐ Baptism
☐ Membership
☐ Life Groups
☐ Baby Dedication
☐ Offering Envelopes
☐ what it means to become a follower of Jesus Christ
☐ next steps as a new follower of Jesus Christ
☐ opportunities to serve
☐ general information

☐ Mr ☐ Mrs ☐ Miss ☐ Ms

Name: _____

Address: _____

_____

City: _____

Postal Code: _____

Phone: _____

Email: _____

☐ Address change
☐ Please add to next directory
☐ Please provide a mail folder

Lots going on at this church

This is a great church with lots happening— so much in fact that I think it would have served them well to make their Communication Card a separate piece, especially since it is right next to the Sermon Notes and if you mess up tearing it off, you could mess up your Sermon Notes.

A relatively simple bulletin and design, but effective. The copy here does not due it justice as the bulletin was printed on an almost watercolor quality type paper. They wanted the rendition of the church (and it was beautifully done by a well-known local artist) to be a memento of a visit to the church.

Samples of separate card stock printed connection cards

Here and on the following pages are connection cards printed up separate from the bulletin itself, which I strongly recommend and which I believe are the most likely to be turned in.

BIBLE FAITH CHURCH

PASTORAL CARE CARD

This Card is For the Use Of All Who Attend Bible Faith Church.
If we can help you in some way please let us know. Our pastors and staff want to serve all who need their ministry.

Name_____

Address_____

_____

City_____

Prov_____P.C._____ _____

Ph.Home (____)_____

   Bus. (____)_____

___I am a member ___adherent ___visitor
___Change of address or phone number

My Age Grouping is:
___under 13 yrs.   ___36 - 50 yrs.
___13 - 20 yrs.   ___51 - 65 yrs.
___21 - 35 yrs.   ___over 65 yrs.

I am Interested In:
___becoming a Christian
___New Life Course
___water baptism
___the fullness of the Holy Spirit
___membership information
___a pastoral call
     ___hospital
     ___healing
     ___other
___pre-marital counselling/courses
___baby dedication

(Please give to an usher or place in the offering basket.)

CARING FOR OTHERS

If you know of someone who has been absent from church, is sick or is in need, the pastors would like to know. Please fill in as much as possible of the following and place in the offering basket.

NAME_____

ADDRESS_____

_____

PHONE (____)_____

EXPLANATION_____

_____

_____

_____

_____

My Name is_____

Phone hm(____)_____

   Bus (____)_____

My own effort to contact and encourage

the above is as follows:_____

_____

_____

Serving Others

I wish to volunteer for:_____

_____

Prayer request or special message:

_____

_____

"Bear one another's burdens and so fulfill the law of Christ!" - Galatians 6:2

This card is unique in the second side being about Caring for Others.

You can tell a lot about a church from looking at their connection card and this church clearly cares greatly about serving the needs of people.

Don't try to do too much on your connection card

Though very attractive with the teal ink on bright white paper and a nice selection of typefaces used, this connection card has so much going on, maybe too much.

The most confusing thing to me was the Church Covenant—in very small print on a piece that I am assuming you don't keep, but will give away. What is a person to do? Skim, decide, check a box and get rid of it.

The image, though lovely and I'm sure well loved, makes the small print even harder to read.

One more question: on the front page, there is the question:

"Are you interested in becoming a member of the church?"

—and there are only two replies, yes or no. What if I'm a visitor and have no idea what church membership is even about?

We need to pray through and think through so carefully what we say on our connection cards.

We not only want to get information from folks but we don't want to scare them away or make them feel pressured to make a decision they may not be ready to make.

Great use of a MS Publisher postcard template

I use the postcard templates for connection cards frequently, but this person made it more lively with color and word art for the Welcome! It looks like the sort of happy card that would be fun to fill out and a happy church to connect with.

LUTHERAN CHURCH OF THE MASTER

CONTACT CARD

Welcome!

Date _____

Name _____

Address_____ City _____ State _____ Zip _____

Phone _____ Cell _____ Work _____

E-mail _____

Names and ages of children at home: _____

_____

_____

_____

Please place card at the Welcome Center or hand to an usher. Thank you.   (Over)

I am:

☐ Visitor

☐ Member

I would like:

☐ Church mailings.

☐ To be baptized.

☐ To become a member.

☐ To talk to a minister.

☐ More information about:

_____

_____

_____

Questions or comments:

_____

_____

_____

_____

_____

_____

_____

_____

_____

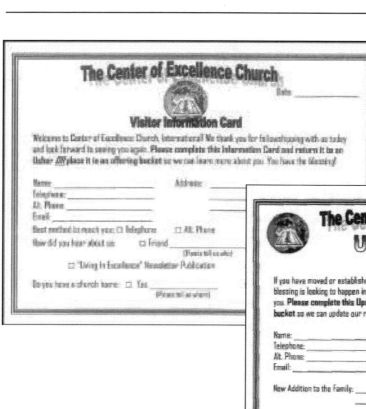

Great idea here—to periodically give out a different colored UPDATE CARD. If you have the printed book, not the e-book, you may not see the color change, but it's there. Yes, people are supposed to update the church every week, but they get distracted or forget, and this is an effective reminder.

Simple and clear, this gets the job done. The only change I would make on this is to not do it up on such dark paper.

We read best when there is high contrast between the print and the paper. It's easy to get bored in the church office and want to print on colored paper to liven things up, but black print on white paper is the easiest on the eyes.

Special event sign-in cards examples

In addition to making it a priority to use Connection Cards effectively every week, special events provide a unique opportunity to make connections.

Sadly, so many churches work very hard to put on a seasonal celebration or special event and often hundreds of strangers to the church come to the event. However, if they only attend that event and never come back again, there is tremendous lost potential to make lasting connections with your church and ultimately to Jesus.

A Connection Card is a natural and important way to make sure the impact of your special event lasts beyond the event itself.

Sign-in cards for special events don't have to be fancy, you just have to make a connection.

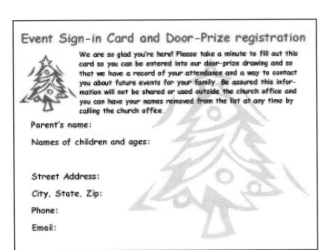

If appropriate, you can offer a prize drawing as an incentive for filling them out, for example:

- A big pumpkin filled with Halloween goodies.

- An Easter basket filled with Easter Candy.

- A giant Christmas stocking filled with yummy treats.

- A gift certificate appropriate to the holiday.

If you wanted to do more than one gift, you might get donations from local businesses.

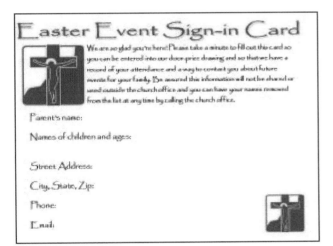

Be sure to follow up immediately on Special Event Connection Cards.

Keep in mind the advice given previously in this book on follow up. Some additional tips for Special Event Connection Card follow up:

• A postcard is a perfect follow-up tool—no one has to bother with opening it up to get the message. Whatever method you choose, be sure to:

Make your special or seasonal event more than simply one great time of celebration. Create, promote, and follow-up on special event connection cards for all the work and prayers of your special event to have lasting impact.

• Thank people for coming.

• Let them know what other seasonal events you have coming up.

• Consider sending additional cards with encouraging tips, ideas, for how to celebrate the holidays.

• Send additional invitations.

• DO NOT worry about being bothersome—marketing companies know it takes many repetitions for people to remember your message and to respond.

• Your message is far more important than the latest consumer product, so be persistent

Though you are more than welcome to use these any of these examples as inspiration, on the website: **www.effectivechurchcom.com** are download-able templates in Microsoft Publisher for Effective Church Communication Members that you can modify and use to create your own cards.

Production note on Special Event Connection Cards

Be sure to print them on heavy-duty card stock (60# to 110# is recommended) so they are easy to hold and fill out. In addition, be sure you print them using an ink-based system, so people can write on the image. This is a perfect job for a digital duplicator.

Below are some of the more recent examples of connection cards on the ECC site, we are constantly adding new ones you can access through the TEMPLATE link on the home page of: www.effectivechurchcom.com.

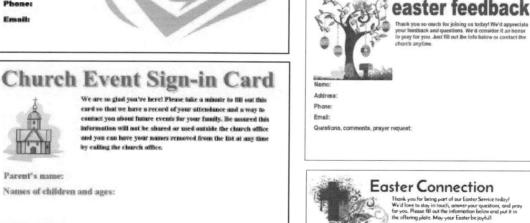

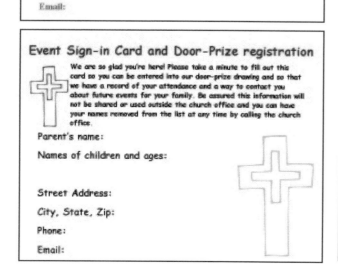

Prayer Card Examples to give out at special events

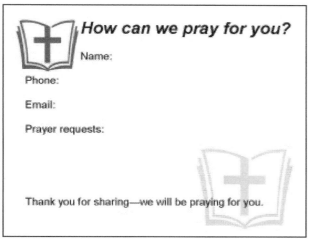

Sometimes at special events, Sunday School classes, or small groups, one of the best ways to connect with people is to ask how you can pray for them.

My husband and I have found this to be one of the most effective ways to form firm bonds with people and to grow a ministry.

Almost any situation is an appropriate one in which you can ask if people want prayer. You'll be amazed at how open people will be.

You can follow up with a note, email or call or simply a personal comment when you see them next to let them know that you are praying for them.

Though you are more than welcome to use these examples as inspiration, on the website: www.effectivechurchcom.com are downloadable templates so that you can modify and print your own cards.

CHAPTER TWELVE

Software recommendation for creating communication cards

Many of the connection cards that I create I do in MS Publisher because it is so easy to do them in it.

Especially for the simple prayer request cards that are printed 4 per page, you can use the Postcard Template in MS Publisher. You simply create one card as the example below shows; then tell it to print 4 per page and it will lay them out, space them and you are done with it.

The screen shot below and the ones on the following page illustrate this.

NOTE: when you read this you may be using a newer or different version of MS Publisher, but the basic process is the same.

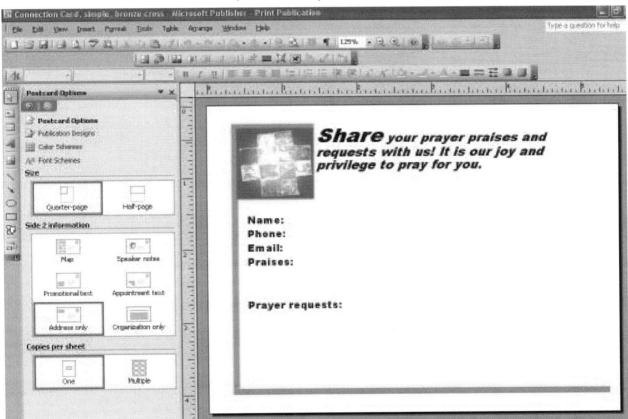

Above is a prayer request connection card being created in MS Publisher. As you can see on the side, I am doing it up in the Postcard Template that will create 4 postcards per page.

If I had a larger graphic image or wanted to ask for more information, I could also use the publication option of creating it on a half-page.

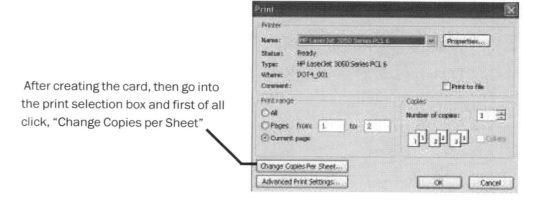

After creating the card, then go into the print selection box and first of all click, "Change Copies per Sheet"

Be sure "Print multiple copies per sheet" is checked and then you'll get a printout like the one below.

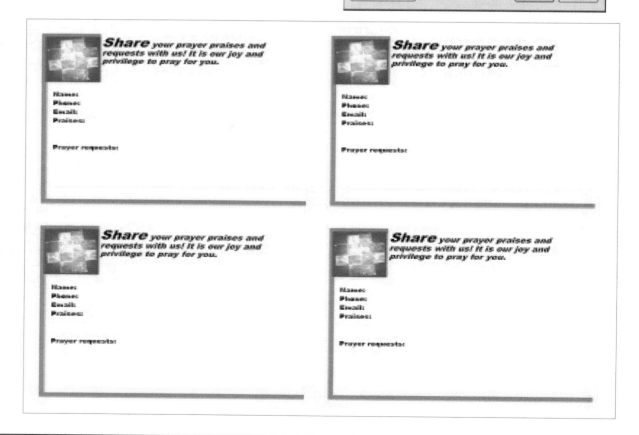

CHAPTER THIRTEEN

Hardware considerations for creating communication cards

As the cards above illustrate, if you want to use an image behind your connection cards, either your church logo for branding, a message or an overall image, you must use an ink-based printing system so people can write on them.

In the actual production of your communication cards, there are some very important factors you must keep in mind:

· You need to be able to produce the cards quickly, cheaply, and in large quantities because the entire congregation gets them every week.

· You need to produce them on lightweight card stock, because for the reasons listed earlier in the book you will get a much better response if you do that.

· You have to be able to write on the cards with the inexpensive pens and pencils many churches have available in the pews.

The last factor seems very obvious, but it isn't in the practical production of many communication products I've seen come out of churches. The reason is that so many churches today produce their communications on color copiers or color lasers. These machines product gorgeous, full-color images, they produce them using toner and you can't write on toner, because it is slick.

You need to print your communication cards with an ink-based print system because ink sinks into the paper and you can write over it. This is especially important if the church wants to print their logo or some sort of Christian image behind the lines upon which you want people to write. The bottom line is that color copiers and laser machines are not good to use to create communication cards. What then is?

Great machines to produce communication cards, quickly and inexpensively are ink-based digital duplicators and the RISO ComColor Injet Printer.

An ink-based printing system meets all the requirements listed above. The best machines to do these are digital duplicators or what I currently recommend is the RISO ComColor Injet Printer. You could do them with your desktop inkjet printer, but the cost and slowness of these machines makes them impractical for all but the shortest print runs.

Digital duplicators and the newer ComColor Printer are great workhorse production machines for churches. They do not do the kind of high quality image you get from a color laser copier, but they are a fraction of the cost to purchase and a tiny, tiny fraction of the cost to operate. The color copier is fantastic for quality PR communications, but for forms and the large number of connection cards you need each week, a digital duplicator or ComColor Printer can be perfect for the job.

In addition digital duplicators or ComColor Printers work well to produce connection cards because, overall they can:

· Produce the cards quickly because there is no heat involved in laying down ink on paper in contrast to the heat required to fuse the image with a toner-based copier. It also means you can do lengthy runs without overheating or jamming.

· Lightweight card stock feeds through the machines well in the ones that have a straight paper path, so you won't get jams.

To find them a good digital duplicator or ComColor Injet Printer, the most helpful recommendation that I could give you now is twofold:

One, trust your local office equipment dealer

The person who can help you the most is always the person who works for a company that keeps the priority of the church in mind. I know many, many dealers that I have had the privilege of working with in the years that I traveled and taught seminars, who truly work very hard to serve the church customers that they have.

Your long term trusting relationship with a dealer is the best guarantee of good equipment.

Two, make sure they understand your need for a non-toner-based machine for this work

You probably need more than one machine to do all the print production work you need done in the church, meaning both a copier and a digital duplicator, but a good sales professional can help you select the machines that will cost less overall and do the kind of work you need for the different publications you create.

Many sales people and dealers who work with churches assume that all of the reproduction needs of the church involve high quality color these days—assuming churches want more impact, etc. in their ministry outreach materials.

Though that may be true for many things you produce in the church office, connection cards are unique because they are more of a workhorse, service piece that is produced in large quantities and requires that people be able to write on it. In addition, many of the publications you produce for children's ministry and teaching ministries also do not need high color or toner-based quality.

The bottom line production reality for connection cards, and many other work horse publications produced by the church is that fancy high end quality isn't the most important characteristic needed in a machine—fast, inexpensive production is. In most churches the combination of a digital duplicator and a copier takes care of all the church printing needs. It isn't a matter of one machine or the other, both do different jobs well to support the total print production needs of a church.

Share with your dealer this chapter and any other parts of this book you think might be useful to help them understand your needs. With your purchase of this book, you have my permission to make copies from it, to help your church and those serving it, with no copyright guilt involved.

The hardest work is ahead

Setting up an effective ministry using connection cards is a huge amount of work. Getting the vision, procedures, communications, and people in place is exhausting. But as difficult as these tasks are, the hardest one is ahead of you and that is because the biggest challenge to a successful connection card ministry is to be consistent. Consistency over the long term is needed in:

· Creating the cards every week.

· Putting them into the bulletin every week.

· Collecting, triaging, sorting and making certain cards get to the proper people for recording and follow up.

· Prompt and personalized follow-up—completing the connection.

Consistency is also needed in:

· Presenting them to the congregation each week in an exciting upbeat way.

· Giving people time each week to fill them out.

· Praying for prayer requests and responses each week.

· Reminding staff and volunteers of the incredible importance of the connections made.

Let me warn you, there will be times when every fiber of your being will scream that these cards are unnecessary; there will be weeks when the copier will jam (if you don't have an ink-based printer); there will often be someone who loudly proclaims that either they are tired of putting them into the bulletins; that people throw half of them on the floor or that they aren't necessary in this age of internet connections when anyone can contact the church anytime through email (forgetting few do and no visitor even knows how).

Rarely a Sunday will go by when it won't seem like you don't have time to pause and give people time to fill them out; when it seems unnecessary to remind people to turn them in, and when, if truth be told, you almost wish nobody would turn one in because then you wouldn't have to deal with them.

On Monday, there will often be an emergency, an email or a phone call that will seem much more important than sorting and triaging the connection cards and responding to them will seem like an unbearable amount of work.

To keep you going when you want to give up on connection cards, the following three reminders may be helpful.

One, important messages require repetition

Every time you get on an airplane, they repeat the same instructions for what seems to be so simple to those who fly a lot: how to put on the seatbelt, what to do in an emergency. They do this because they know that though perhaps 99% of the people have heard it before, if there is an emergency, and if it saves the life of one person, all the repetition will have been worth it. It may seem like you have repeated the same announcement about connection cards and no one is listening, but I promise you that every week there is someone in your church whose spiritual life is in crisis and for whom that announcement might be the difference between eternal life and death.

Jesus describes himself as the Good Shepherd who goes after the one little sheep who has wandered off, while the 99 are safe, doing what they should be doing. That one little sheep needed special attention and Jesus gave it to him and saved his life. When you make the announcement, when you work on the cards, don't do it with a faceless group in mind, but pray that the Lord will enable you to see the ONE person who desperately needs the connection.

Two, there is an a real enemy who wants you to give up

Connection cards and all they can be used to accomplish in your church do not exist in a spiritual vacuum. There is an enemy of our souls who would like nothing better than for visitors to be ignored, for hurting people to be un-touched, for seeking souls to pour out their hearts and then be disappointed because no one responds. That enemy will constantly whisper in your ear that there is never time to announce, collect, or respond to connection cards.

Determine ahead of time to ignore that voice.

Though our enemy is real, we can't blame the enemy for our own sloth and lack of discipline.

Determine ahead of time the procedures for announcing, collecting and responding to connection cards. Make staff accountable for the tasks as-signed. Also, don't forget to share with the entire staff the stories of answered prayers, people getting help, strangers connecting to your church, and the many other wonderful results of consistent and caring use of connection cards.

Three, always remember the eternal consequences of your ministry with connection cards

Consistent, thoughtful use of connection cards **WILL GROW YOUR CHURCH!**

And the eternal destinies of people will be changed.

If you are consistent with your use of them and if you record responses, **you will** see growth in your church, in the number of visitors who return, of people who share prayer requests and praises. But beyond what you see, many of the connections that are made and the eternal destinies that are changed, you may never know about as you work week-by-week to announce, record, and respond to connection cards. To lift your spirit, you need to think about how these cards fit into an eternal picture. To help you do that, let's look at two Bible passages and then a quote from C.S. Lewis; my commentary will follow each.

A snapshot of the final judgement

Many folks fuss and fight over end-times theology, on when and how Jesus will return and bless their hearts, if that is how they want to spend their time, that is between them and Jesus. What does amaze me, however, is how little attention is given to the passages that tell us extremely clearly, no matter what the time line, what is going to happen when we meet Jesus face to face. The first passage is found in Matthew 25:31-46:

When the Son of Man comes in his glory, and all the angels with him, he will sit on his throne in heavenly glory. All the nations will be gathered before him, and he will separate the people one from another as a shepherd separates the sheep from the goats. He will put the sheep on his right and the goats on his left.

"Then the King will say to those on his right, 'Come, you who are blessed by my Father; take your inheritance, the kingdom prepared for you since the creation of the world. For I was hungry and you gave me something to eat, I was thirsty and you gave me something to drink, I was a stranger and you invited me in, I needed clothes and you clothed me, I was sick and you looked after me, I was in prison and you came to visit me.'

"Then the righteous will answer him, 'Lord, when did we see you hungry and feed you, or thirsty and give you something to drink? When did we see you a stranger and invite you in, or needing clothes and clothe you? When did we see you sick or in prison and go to visit you?'

"The King will reply, 'I tell you the truth, whatever you did for one of the least of these brothers of mine, you did for me.'

"Then he will say to those on his left, 'Depart from me, you who are cursed, into the eternal fire prepared for the devil and his angels. For I was hungry and you gave me nothing to eat, I was thirsty and you gave me nothing to drink, I was a stranger and you did not invite me in, I needed clothes and you did not clothe me, I was sick and in prison and you did not look after me.'

"They also will answer, 'Lord, when did we see you hungry or thirsty or a stranger or needing clothes or sick or in prison, and did not help you?'

"He will reply, 'I tell you the truth, whatever you did not do for one of the least of these, you did not do for me.'

"Then they will go away to eternal punishment, but the righteous to eternal life."

Commentary:

Let's get practical about this passage. It is very important to Jesus how we meet the needs of those hungry, hurting, ill, and in prison. It is so important that Jesus says to meet those needs, he counts as the same as ministering to him personally. Also, to not meet those needs means to reject him and if people reject him on earth, he rejects them in heaven. Very harsh words indeed.

But how we might ask can we find out about the needs of people? How can we practically connect with them and meet their needs?

At the final judgement of all things, Jesus doesn't ask about your denomination; your view of end-times theology, he doesn't even ask if you voted Democrat or Republican, which might be a bit of a surprise to many (it is an election year as I write this).

What he will want to know is—how did you meet the needs of hungry, hurting, sick, isolated people?

Your consistent ministry of connection cards will enable you to respond with joy at that time.

We need to view these little cards and their cries for help as personal requests from Jesus.

It isn't the only way, and I pray your church has many outreach ministries in place, but one way every church can do this is through your connection cards. As stated earlier in this book—when tragedy and needs happen, people go to church. Often they will fill out that little card. We need to view these little cards and their cries for help as personal requests from Jesus. We also need to remember that to ignore the needs of hurting people is the same as to ignore a personal plea from Jesus.

From this passage, it appears that's the way he views it. May Jesus have mercy on us all for the times we have failed and may we all commit to a faithful response to connect with people and to meet their needs in the future.

Response is required, no matter what your resources

Not every church can respond to every need in the same way. You may be one person starting a church or a singles' class and you want to connect with and meet the needs of your people. Or you might be on staff of a large or mega-church and though you reach thousands in your services each week, you might have the nagging feeling that people's needs are falling through the cracks. Whatever your resources, you are responsible to make the most of them as this passage in Matt. 25:14-30 shows:

> *"Again, it will be like a man going on a journey, who called his servants and entrusted his property to them. To one he gave five talents of money, to another two talents, and to another one talent, each according to his ability. Then he went on his journey. The man who had received the five talents went at once and put his money to work and gained five more. So also, the one with the two talents gained two more. But the man who had received the one talent went off, dug a hole in the ground and hid his master's money.*

> *"After a long time the master of those servants returned and settled accounts with them. The man who had received the five talents brought the other five. 'Master,' he said, 'you entrusted me with five talents. See, I have gained five more.'*

> *"His master replied, 'Well done, good and faithful servant! You have been faithful with a few things; I will put you in charge of many things. Come and share your master's happiness!'*

> *"The man with the two talents also came. 'Master,' he said, 'you entrusted me with two talents; see, I have gained two more.'*

> *"His master replied, 'Well done, good and faithful servant! You have been faithful with a few things; I will put you in charge of many things. Come and share your master's happiness!'*

> *"Then the man who had received the one talent came. 'Master,' he said, 'I knew that you are a hard man, harvesting where you have not sown and gathering where you have not scattered seed. So I was afraid and went out and hid your talent in the ground. See, here is what belongs to you.'*

"His master replied, 'You wicked, lazy servant! So you knew that I harvest where I have not sown and gather where I have not scattered seed? Well then, you should have put my money on deposit with the bankers, so that when I returned I would have received it back with interest.

"'Take the talent from him and give it to the one who has the ten talents. For everyone who has will be given more, and he will have an abundance. Whoever does not have, even what he has will be taken from him. And throw that worthless servant outside, into the darkness, where there will be weeping and gnashing of teeth."

Commentary:

Make the most of what you have. If you are a huge church, with immense resources, make certain you make the most of them. If you are a tiny church or a person alone with a passion to reach people and help them mature in the faith, make the most of that.

Having either too many people to keep track of or too few resources to reach out doesn't work as an excuse.

Some additional thoughts about a focus on eternity, from *Mere Christianity* by C.S. Lewis

Though looking to the future and our hope of heaven is important motivation, C.S. Lewis had a wonderful way of tying in future hope with practical actions on earth:

Hope. . .means that a continual looking forward to the eternal world is not (as some modern people think) a form of escapism or wishful thinking, but one of the things a Christian is meant to do. It does not mean that we are to leave the present world as it is. If you read history you will find that the Christians who did most for this present world were just those who thought most of the next. The Apostles themselves, who set foot on the conversion of the Roman Empire, the great men who built up the Middle Ages, the English Evangelicals who abolished the Slave Trade, all left their mark on Earth, precisely because their minds were occupied with Heaven. It is since Christians have largely ceased to think of the other world that they have become so ineffective in this. Aim at Heaven and you will get earth "thrown in": aim at earth and you will get neither.

Commentary:

If you have an eternal view of the importance of individuals and if you do the repetitive word of announcing, recording, and responding to connection cards and effectively use them as a tool in your church, needs will be met, your church will grow in numbers, and your people will progress in Christian maturity.

To remain effective and consistent in our ministry with connection cards, not only do we need to look expansively into eternity, but we also need to not ignore the little things because......

The little things are often what God uses for his glory

This goes against almost everything in us and in our culture today. We admire the big, the bold move, the mega whatever whether it is in movie stars, athletes or media. Even in the church we are drawn to of mega-churches and their conferences and resources that are designed to train and inspire, but often result in a futile attempt to copy a system that worked because of the uniqueness of the leader or the culture or any number of other reasons.

None of us are immune to this cultural desire to think that if we do some really big thing that people will notice and respond. I confess to that fighting that desire as I started work on this book. I have many boxes and piles of material on all sorts of subjects that after thirty-some years of working in church communications I know might be of use to other church communicators. The question was, where to start, which area to work on first? Communication leadership, bulletins, type, design, writing, newsletters—I have material on all of these topics and many more.

To complicate my decision I've recently learned to do things with blogging and websites and really wanted to start there. I want to appear "relevant" and "with it" or whatever term is in vogue today, though I laugh at myself, even as I write that as if writing about websites and blogs would make a sixty-something lady who lives in a trailer "with it."

What I constantly returned to in my quiet times with the Lord is that what I knew church communicators really needed was help with the basics, the little things that form the foundation of connecting with people and of church communications. From years of personal ministry I knew that connection cards are the essential start for many ministries in the church. The following verses keep coming back to me:

> 'Not by might nor by power, but by my Spirit,' says the LORD Almighty (Zac. 4:6).

> God chose the foolish things of the world to shame the wise; God chose the weak things of the world to shame the strong. He chose the lowly things of this world and the despised things—and the things that are not—to nullify the things that are, so that no one may boast before him (I Cor. 1:27-29).

I knew as I thought about those verses, that God is pleased to use for his glory seemingly little things. In obedience I've written this book and offer it up to you with my prayers that you will take seriously the ministry of connection cards, that you will be strengthened and encouraged as you create them, that your cards will connect your church with people, meet needs, and help people grow to maturity in Jesus.

Finally I pray you will be faithful and consistent. Week in, week out, treating every announcement, recording, and follow-up with the upmost care because what you do in your connection card ministry can bring many people to Jesus and give you great joy when you meet him face-to-face.

CHAPTER FIFTEEN

Additional resources

A number of additional resources for effective Connection Card ministry, including templates and an instructional video with a PDF handout for notes is available for members at: www.effectivechurchcom.com.

UPDATE NOTE: please go to the site and put in the search box "Connection Cards." We are in the process of updating and adding a lot of material to this topic, so some items may look a little different when you see them.

Membership in the Effective Church Communications website gives you access to training videos with PDF notes and editable templates for creating church communication cards.

Join today for access for these and many other resources!

Go to:
www.effectivechurchcom.com/ecc-membership/

Membership in this website entitles you to access of many training videos, hundreds of ready-to-print church communications, Editable MS Publisher Templates and a Library of e-books on church communications. Membership is only $9.99 a month or $99 a year and a church can share ONE membership. Please go to: www.effectivechurchcom.com/ecc-membership/ to sign up.
It is one of the best investments you can make for the effectiveness of the communication program for your church.

Encouragement from other church communicators

In addition to the training information above, the website also has articles and answers to questions about various church communication pieces. The following article is based on a question sent in to me.

Connection Cards: church service distraction or great ministry tool?

I recently received the following email (only slightly edited for privacy) with a practical ministry question about Connection Cards and how to avoid the time filling out the cards and collecting them more than an awkward break in the service. Following the email, I have some advice, but PLEASE add your comments and practices in the comment section that follows.

Question about Connection Cards

I have a question or two concerning having the whole congregation fill out connection cards during the service time. I know you believe this a very important part of the Sunday morning church service. I have read several church leaders that agree.

I am Director of Administration for our church and have approached our Senior Pastor about doing this. He has been the pastor for 25 years so he is a very experienced pastor. When I first mentioned us possibly doing this he said he could not imagine having a break in the service where pretty much everything comes to a standstill while hundreds of people fill out these cards. He said he would think it would be a real "flow" breaker if you know what I mean...however he cares more about doing what is best for the body of our church than not wanting to try something new. So, he is willing to give this a try but I have a couple of questions that I'd like to ask you so I will have more information to approach him with...

What would you estimate the time to be to complete these cards? Each service would have around 200 people in it....Would you estimate 2 or 3 minutes or something much shorter like 30 seconds?

Also, when other churches do this do they have something going on at the same time or does everything come to a standstill while they are being filled out?

My answer

Thanks so much for your question! These are very important concerns.

Before I answer directly about the time it takes, allow me to make some preliminary comments that will set the foundation for the practical application. In some ways this is the church communication equivalent of laying out the orthodoxy of belief as to why do the cards at all and their purpose in the ministry of the church before the orthopraxy of implementation.

A Biblical basis for Connection Cards

Connection Cards are an essential part of shepherding your flock, which is a primary command to who lead in the church:

Be shepherds of God's flock that is under your care, watching over them—not because you must, but because you are willing, as God wants you to be; not pursuing dishonest gain, but eager to serve.
1 Peter 5:2

Serving as a shepherd requires many skills and great dependence on the Lord, but a foundation for all our shepherding involves knowing the status of your flock.

Be sure you know the condition of your flocks;
give careful attention to your herds. Prov. 27:23

A theme throughout the prophets as God challenged his people to repent prior to the judgment of captivity, was that the spiritual leaders, the shepherds were not doing their job. Here is one description of this situation:

Israel's watchmen are blind,
they all lack knowledge;
they are all mute dogs,
they cannot bark;
they lie around and dream,
they love to sleep. Isaiah 56:10

With hundreds of people in the average church service today, it is physically impossible for a pastor, or even a group of leaders to personally meet with every visitor or to check with every member to see how they are doing. But with Connection Cards—when presented with genuine care and a desire to connect with visitors and to find out the prayer requests and concerns of everyone attending—far from being a break in the service, they become a tangible witness to the care and love of the church for the people.

With them you can connect with visitors, find out about needs, be updated on prayer requests and notified of new ones.

Practical issues in collecting connection cards

Now that we've established a basis for the importance of the cards. As with anything else, the response of your people to anything in the service depends greatly on how it is presented by the worship leader. The book on <u>Connection Cards</u> has some extended advice on this topic, here it is:

At an early point in the worship service, the leader says something like this:

We want to welcome you to our service! We care about each and every one of you—if you are here for the first time or a long-time member. We care about your questions, your concerns, your needs. At this point in the service, we use our connection card to share that information. We'll play some music and while we are doing that, please take out the card and fill it out. I'm going to take a minute to write out my prayer requests for the week, as you write yours. Hold on to the card and if, at any time during the service if you have a question or comment, write it down. We'll collect them at the end of the service.

Then literally time it to see how long it takes to fill out the basic information you ask for on the card and to write a brief question or comment—much of that will depend on how complex you make the card. I will most likely take under a minute.

You can collect them shortly after this announcement if you collect the offering early in the service, however another option will get a greater response. In the book I give a much longer explanation of this, but if possible and for the greatest impact, wait until the end of the service to take up the cards and the offering. Prior to the collection, say something like this:

After hearing the message today, if you have a question, a comment, a prayer request, if there is any way we can be of service to you in your search for God or Christian walk, we want to know about it. We'll be taking up the offering in a minute and if you are a visitor—we don't want any money from you—all we want is that connection card!

If you do what I've just suggested—be prepared! You will be amazed at how people pour out their hearts if you give them the time, opportunity, and encouragement to do this. In the book on Connection Cards, there is an entire chapter on how to be prepared for the response you will get. Preparation for a timely response is vital before you make any changes in how you use Connection Cards, because to encourage people to share and not to get a response is heart-breaking.

Finally, far from being an interruption or break in the flow of a service, when used intentionally, joyfully, and backed by prayer, the time encouraging people to fill out Connection Cards can be one of the most valuable shepherding experiences in your church.

CHAPTER SIXTEEN

End notes and information about ECC & Yvon Prehn

End notes, Reprint Information, Resources, etc.

Permission to reproduce material:

You may reproduce any of the content in this book for your church staff or you may reprint it in any publication or website that is intended to help churches without additional permission and with my blessings.

PLEASE use the following citation:
by Yvon Prehn, www.effectivechurchcom.com

I would appreciate you linking to my website and/or letting me know if you cite me, but if ministry life is just too crazy to take time to do that, instead, have a latte, relax, and forget it.

Interview info:

If you would like to interview me on any of the topics in this book or any related to church communications for either print articles or other media, I'd be happy to chat—contact me through yvon@effectivechurchcom.com. I have done extensive radio work, some television, and am comfortable with unscripted interviews, call-in, and talk formats.

Additional resources, training and church communication instruction:

The website: www.effectivechurchcom.com has hundreds of articles, videos, podcasts and additional resources to help you grow as an effective church communicator. The website has both free materials, plus low-cost downloadable communication helps, and materials available to members only,

Effective Church Communications also has many books for sale in paperback and Kindle format at amazon.com (just search for Yvon Prehn).

Citation note:

Some of these articles appeared in earlier versions in either articles in *Christian Computing Magazine*, my book, *The Heart of Church Communications*, misc. books and reprints, or on my website, www.effectivechurchcom.com.

Scripture versions and citations:

Unless otherwise noted, Bible verses are from the New International Version. Scripture taken from the HOLY BIBLE, NEW INTERNATIONAL VERSION®. Copyright © 1973, 1978, 1984 International Bible Society. Used by permission of Zondervan. All rights reserved.

Comments, corrections, questions, suggestions for additional articles or information to help church communications etc.

Please send to yvon@effectivechurchcom.com

About Yvon Prehn

Yvon Prehn is the founder, director, and primary content creator of the training site for church communicators: http://www.effectivechurchcom.com, a website that provides practical training in print and digital communications to help churches fully fulfill the Great Commission. Yvon has degrees in English and education, a MA in Church History, in addition to attending seminary and doing graduate work in Communications.

Yvon has worked in communication ministry for over 35 years. She was a free-lance newspaper reporter and religion writer for the *Colorado Springs SUN.* When desktop publishing was first invented, Yvon was a top-rated, national trainer in desktop publishing for Padgett/Thompson, the nation's largest one-day seminar company and she wrote the first book on desktop publishing for the church, *The Desktop Publishing Remedy.*

She worked as a communications consultant and trainer for many of the ministries headquartered in Colorado Springs and was senior editor at Compassion International and Young Life International. For over twenty years (fourteen full-time) she traveled all over North America teaching seminars on church communications to thousands of church communicators.

Yvon has written for many of the major Christian magazines and has written many books on church communications available at the links below. Currently, Yvon is not traveling, but creating articles, books, videos, podcasts, and other materials to educate, equip, and inspire church communicators. She is available for radio and podcast interviews and gives free reprints of materials to any church or Christian group that asks for them. She can also provide specialized webinars and DVD training for ministries or church conferences.

Yvon and her husband Paul, live in Ventura, California, where Yvon teaches an adult Bible class and puts into practice what she teaches creating communications for it and other ministries.

For additional resources for Effective Church Communications and to connect with Yvon Prehn:

- Yvon Prehn's email: yvon@effectivechurchcom.com
- Effective Church Communications website, ebooks, and blog: www.effectivechurchcom.com
- Yvon Prehn's Print books on amazon: www.amazon.com/s/ref=ntt_athr_dp_sr_1?_encoding=UTF8&sort=relevancerank&search-alias=books&field-author=Yvon%20Prehn
- Facebook: www.facebook.com/EffectiveChurchCommunications
- YouTube videos: www.youtube.com/yvonprehn
- LinkedIN: www.linkedin.com/in/yvonprehn
- Pinterest: www.pinterest.com/yvonprehn
- Smashwords: www.smashwords.com/profile/view/yvonprehn

Notes and Applications

Notes and Applications

Made in the USA
Columbia, SC
05 January 2024

29951725R00063